I0121697

Misguided Democracy in Malaysia and Indonesia

Misguided Democracy in Malaysia and Indonesia

Digital Propaganda in Southeast Asia

Nuurrianti Jalli and Ika Idris

LEXINGTON BOOKS
Lanham • Boulder • New York • London

Rowman & Littlefield
Bloomsbury Publishing Inc, 1359 Broadway, New York, NY 10018, USA
Bloomsbury Publishing Plc, 50 Bedford Square, London, WC1B 3DP, UK
Bloomsbury Publishing Ireland, 29 Earlsfort Terrace, Dublin 2, D02 AY28, Ireland
www.bloomsbury.com

Published by Lexington Books
An imprint of The Rowman & Littlefield Publishing Group, Inc.
4501 Forbes Boulevard, Suite 200, Lanham, Maryland 20706
www.rowman.com
86-90 Paul Street, London EC2A 4NE

Copyright © 2024 by Strategic Information and Research Development Centre

All rights reserved. No part of this publication may be: i) reproduced or transmitted in
any form, electronic or mechanical, including photocopying, recording or by means
of any information storage or retrieval system without prior permission in writing from
the publishers; or ii) used or reproduced in any way for the training, development or
operation of artificial intelligence (AI) technologies, including generative AI technologies.
The rights holders expressly reserve this publication from the text and data mining
exception as per Article 4(3) of the Digital Single Market Directive (EU) 2019/790.

British Library Cataloguing in Publication Information available

Library of Congress Cataloging-in-Publication Data

Names: Jalli, Nuurrianti, author. | Idris, Ika, author.
Title: Misguided democracy in Malaysia and Indonesia : digital propaganda in Southeast
    Asia / Nuurrianti Jalli and Ika Idris.
Description: Lanham : Lexington Books, [2024] | Includes bibliographical references and index.
Identifiers: LCCN 2023035417 (print) | LCCN 2023035418 (ebook) |
    ISBN 9781666925258 (cloth) | ISBN 9781666925265 (ebook)
Subjects: LCSH: Disinformation—Malaysia. | Disinformation—Indonesia. |
    Propaganda—Malaysia. | Propaganda—Indonesia. | Digital media—Political
    aspects—Malaysia. | Digital media—Political aspects—Indonesia. | Digital
    media— Social aspects—Malaysia. | Digital media—Social aspects—Indonesia.
Classification: LCC HM1231 .J355 2024 (print) | LCC HM1231 (ebook) |
    DDC 302.23/109595—dc23/eng/20230811
LC record available at https://lccn.loc.gov/2023035417
LC ebook record available at https://lccn.loc.gov/2023035418

To our families;

To my late father, Jalli bin Sahari, whose passion for learning instilled in me an insatiable pursuit of knowledge, this work carries a piece of you. To my mother, Mary Jini, your embodiment of resilience and grit continues to be my guiding light. To my late grandmother, Rabiah binti Abdullah, your love has been the nurturing force that has shaped me into the woman I am today. And to my husband, Rafiq Darwis bin Mohammad, your tireless support and unwavering belief in me, even during the most challenging phases of this endeavor, has been my steadfast anchor. —Nuurrianti Jalli

This book is dedicated to Mika and Aidan, who chatted about the history of the world war and propaganda during dinner time. —Ika Idris

Contents

List of Figures

Preface

Nuurrianti Jalli

In an age characterized by rapid technological advancements and ever-growing interconnectedness, the Internet has undeniably transformed every facet of our lives. From the ways we communicate, work, and learn to how we participate in the political sphere, the digital revolution has reshaped the very fabric of our societies. This book, *Misguided Democracy in Malaysia and Indonesia: Digital Propaganda in Southeast Asia*, delves into the darker side of these transformations, exploring the intersection of the Internet, democracy, and propaganda in Southeast Asia.

Southeast Asia, a diverse and vibrant region, has experienced a remarkable surge in Internet penetration and social media usage in the last two decades. This growth has not only changed the way people connect and share ideas but has also provided fertile ground for the dissemination of disinformation and the manipulation of public opinion. In this book, we aim to provide a comprehensive examination of how the Internet has been weaponized by various actors to spread propaganda, with a particular focus on Malaysia, Indonesia, and other countries in the region.

Throughout the chapters, we will examine the strategies and tactics employed by propagandists, state actors, and political parties to exploit the affordances of the Internet and social media platforms. From fabricated news articles and doctored images to targeted disinformation campaigns, the book will provide an in-depth analysis of the myriad ways in which digital tools are used to mislead and manipulate public opinion.

The book also seeks to illuminate the consequences of this widespread dissemination of disinformation on the democratic processes in Southeast Asia. With elections increasingly influenced by online propaganda, we explore the impact of such tactics on voter behavior, political discourse, and social cohesion, as well as the potential implications for regional stability and international relations. In addition to providing a thorough exploration of the phenomenon of online propaganda in the region, *Misguided Democracy* discusses the challenges faced by governments, civil society organizations, and technology companies in addressing the issue. The book delves into the delicate balance between combating disinformation and safeguarding freedom of speech, examining the roles and responsibilities of various stakeholders in promoting transparency, accountability, and digital literacy.

As you embark on this journey through the complex and often murky world of Internet propaganda in Southeast Asia, we hope that *Misguided Democracy* will not only shed light on the challenges facing the region's democracies but also inspire thoughtful reflection on the role of the Internet and social media in shaping the future of our societies. Ultimately, it is our collective responsibility to ensure that the digital revolution serves as a force for good, empowering citizens to engage in informed and constructive democratic processes.

Acknowledgments

In the journey of penning this book, we have found ourselves standing on the shoulders of many who have generously offered their support, encouragement, and wisdom. For this, we are forever grateful.

Firstly, we want to acknowledge our beloved families, our parents, spouses, and children, who were our rocks during this grueling process. The love, support, and understanding they offered allowed us to burn the midnight oil, spend days buried in research, and traverse the winding paths of writing this book. A particular mention goes to Jalli bin Sahari and Rabiah binti Abdullah, the father and grandmother of Nuurrianti Jalli, who sadly passed away during this journey. Their memory continues to inspire us.

A special note of thanks goes to our mentor, Prof. Drew McDaniel. Your guidance, wisdom, and belief in our scholarly pursuit since our doctoral years have been pivotal in shaping our research. Your passion for media and Southeast Asian studies continues to inspire us.

We also want to express our appreciation to our dedicated colleagues at Oklahoma State University and Monash University Indonesia. We'd like to thank them for their insightful critiques, stimulating discussions, and constant encouragement. We're grateful for their diverse perspectives and intellectual curiosity, both within and outside our academic circles.

Over the years, our collaborations with practitioners in the industry, from local to international organizations, have gifted us with valuable insights that have influenced this book.

To you, our readers, thank you for your interest and for giving our work a purpose. We sincerely hope this book enriches your understanding and sparks a deeper interest in digital propaganda in Southeast Asia, particularly in Malaysia and Indonesia. If any questions arise as you read the book, we are happy to have a conversation with you via email or online dialogue.

To everyone mentioned and those we may have overlooked, please accept our humble gratitude. Any shortcomings in this book are entirely our own.

With sincere thanks,
Nuurrianti Jalli and Ika Idris

Chapter 1

Understanding Propaganda

When the topic of propaganda arises, many people's minds immediately turn to the World Wars, neglecting the reality that propaganda is ubiquitous, especially in today's interconnected world. From radio ads and amusing TikTok videos to Netflix TV shows and social media news, propaganda is all around us (Heller, 2021). In this highly connected age, the Internet has become a powerful tool for individuals to disseminate information with specific agendas, reaching audiences worldwide. The concept of "propaganda" boasts a long history as one of the oldest methods of public persuasion.

In this chapter, we will investigate the multifaceted nature of propaganda, tracing its historical definitions and contemporary interpretations while focusing on its various forms and applications within the Southeast Asian context. We will also examine the rhetorical modality of propaganda, which will aid in understanding the significance of rhetoric in shaping persuasive messages. Subsequently, we will delve into the relationship between human psychology and propaganda, exploring how psychological factors can make individuals more susceptible to manipulation. Finally, we will analyze a range of propaganda techniques, supported by contemporary examples from Southeast Asia, to illustrate the diverse methods employed by propagandists. The primary objective of this chapter is to enrich your understanding of propaganda and provide a comprehensive overview of its evolution and presence in public life throughout history.

PROPAGANDA: WHAT IS IT ALL ABOUT?

Up until the end of the sixteenth century, the concept of propaganda and its related forms were primarily associated with biology, referring to the reproduction of plants and animals (Fellows, 1959). However, during the sixteenth century, the term "propaganda," derived from the Latin phrase "which ought to be propagated," began to denote the act of spreading Catholic doctrine to non-Christian lands through the establishment of de propaganda fide, a commission consisting of three cardinals appointed by Pope Gregory XIII (1572–1585) (Fellow, 1959).

The term "propaganda" first appeared in the English language in 1718, retaining its religious connotation, and persisted in this context through the eighteenth and nineteenth centuries. Nevertheless, during the nineteenth century, the word gradually shifted to encompass political and military agendas, referring to the dissemination of such objectives, though it did not gain widespread popularity until the twentieth century. The First World War (1914–1918) imbued the term with a negative connotation, distancing it from its original religious meaning. Britain's Ministry of Information, the first major state propaganda agency, epitomized the Orwellian notion of directing the thoughts of the masses (Sanders and Taylor, 1982).

Since then, the term "propaganda" has become synonymous with the indoctrination of ideas and strategic disinformation campaigns, employing persuasive tactics with the ultimate aim of shaping public perceptions of the world (Jowett and O'Donnell, 2018).

The term "propaganda" often carries negative connotations, typically referring to the deliberate dissemination of disinformation. While both propaganda and disinformation aim to influence public opinion and behavior, they differ in the nature of the information they employ. Disinformation relies on false or misleading information, intentionally designed to deceive the audience. On the other hand, propaganda may use accurate information but often presents it in a way that appeals to the emotions or biases of the audience, seeking to influence their responses and perspectives.

Various modern definitions of propaganda exist, with several prominent ones featured in scholarly articles. Harold Lasswell (1927) defined propaganda as "the management of collective attitudes by the manipulation of significant symbols" (pg. 627), which later inspired the Institute for Propaganda Analysis' definition: the deliberate expression of opinions or actions by individuals or groups to influence the opinions or actions of others through psychological manipulations (Ross, 2002). Another popular definition by Neil Postman (1993) posits that propaganda is intentionally designed for communication that elicits emotional, immediate, and binary responses, emphasizing the importance of crafting persuasive messages to enhance the effectiveness of propaganda tactics (Fletcher, 1939).

While the various definitions of propaganda may differ depending on the specific goals of the instigators, the core concept remains consistent. What has evolved, however, are the means of communication. Propaganda has been present in early print media through text and visuals, broadcast on television and radio, and now pervades the Internet. As communication technologies continue to change and advance, propaganda adapts accordingly, finding new ways to spread its message. This evolution in communication methods has significantly impacted both the speed and scale of propaganda dissemination.

In this book, we fundamentally regard propaganda as the strategic and methodical employment of persuasive messages to influence the target audience's beliefs, opinions, and behavior concerning the subject matter. Propaganda often appeals to emotions rather than reason through psychological approaches and must encompass the element of intent, where communication is a deliberate effort. In its most effective form, propaganda proactively and significantly impacts the target audience's worldview, as intended by the propagandists. The ultimate goal of the instigators is to shape public opinion, persuade the audience to adopt a position, take action, or even maintain inactivity when confronted with contentious issues.

In Southeast Asia, as in many parts of the world, propaganda has been used negatively by instigators to incite fear and hostility, particularly by employing emotive messages to shape public opinion on socio-political issues (see Joo-Jock, 1976; Wieringa and Nursyahbani, 2018; Armstrong, 2021; Jalli and Idris, 2019; Grant, 1998; Adam, 2016; Heder and Ledgerwood, 2016; Virginie, 2012). During election seasons, orchestrated disinformation campaigns are commonly employed to create misinformed and emotionally driven voters, with the goal of influencing electoral outcomes. However, as mentioned earlier, propaganda is not solely about biased communication objectives; it can also be utilized to encourage action for noble causes. In the Southeast Asian region, propaganda techniques have been employed to raise awareness of social issues, such as human trafficking (see Edna, Ibarra, and McDonald, 2004), to promote collaboration between ASEAN countries in addressing the haze problem (see Jones, 2005; Nguitragool, 2011; Varkkley, 2022), for health campaigns (see Saleh, Azahari, and Ismail, 2013), and to foster a sense of patriotism towards one's nation (see Afifah, Sabardila, and Wahyudi, 2022). See table 1.1.

The Three Colors of Propaganda

Propaganda can also be categorized based on the transparency of its origin and the accuracy of the information (Jowett and O'Donnell, 2018). *White propaganda* is a type wherein the source is easily identifiable, and the information shared is typically accurate. Communication strategists often use white propaganda to present the propagandist or their ally in a favorable light, enhancing credibility and promoting a positive image among the target audience, which ultimately aids in building strong relationships between the

Table 1.1   Positive and Negative Uses of Propaganda in Southeast Asia

Positive Uses of Propaganda	Negative Uses of Propaganda
Propaganda can be employed to champion noble causes as well. In the Southeast Asian region, propaganda techniques have been utilized to raise awareness about human trafficking (see Edna, Ibarra, and McDonald, 2004), encourage collaboration between ASEAN countries to address the haze issue (see Jones, 2005; Nguitragool, 2011; Varkkley, 2022), support health campaigns (see Saleh, Azahari, and Ismail, 2013), and foster a sense of patriotism toward one's nation (see Afifah, Sabardila, and Wahyudi, 2022).	Propaganda is often employed negatively to incite fear and hostility. In every Southeast Asian country, propaganda has been used to negatively influence public opinion on socio-political issues (see Joo-Jock, 1976; Wieringa and Nursyahbani, 2018; Armstrong, 2021; Jalli and Idris, 2019; Grant, 1998; Adam, 2016; Heder and Ledgerwood, 2016; Virginie, 2012). By initiating disinformation campaigns that provoke fear and hostility, a powerful reaction is triggered within civil society, making it a common tactic in the region.

propagandist and the audience. Establishing credibility in this manner can prove beneficial for the propagandist, if not immediately, then at some point in the future.

In contemporary Malaysia and Indonesia, white propaganda is frequently employed by the government to endorse government policies, instill patriotism, and foster national unity in their diverse populations. For instance, in Malaysia, government-funded public service announcements (PSAs) for national unity efforts can be found across various media campaigns, particularly during festive seasons (Ismail, et al., 2021) and in August, when the National Day is celebrated annually on August 31. In Indonesia, white propaganda is often showcased through the production of multiple patriotic films directed by local talents, such as the Habibie and Ainun trilogy (2012–2019), Soekarno (2013), and Jeneral Soedirman (2015) (Maulana and Nugroho, 2018; Yuwita, 2018). Another recent example of white propaganda amid the COVID-19 pandemic is the PSAs produced by government bodies and non-governmental agencies in Malaysia and Indonesia, advocating for vaccination in an effort to improve public health during the crisis.

The second color of propaganda is *black propaganda*, the opposite of the former. The critical characteristics of black propaganda are that the information's source is concealed. It is often misleading, biased, or outright false, and it is intended to misinform the public, to influence public opinion, and to damage the credibility of propagandist's opponents (Jowett and O'Donnell, 2018). In Malaysia and Indonesia, political actors have used black propaganda through the deployments of disinformation campaigns (see table 1.2 for definitions of disinformation, misinformation, and disinformation) over the

Table 1.2   Definitions of Misinformation, Disinformation, and Mal-information

Falseness	Falseness with intent to harm	Intent to Harm
Misinformation is unintentional mistakes such as inaccurate photo captions, dates, statistics, translations, or when satire is taken seriously—spreading false information that the public think is true.	Disinformation is fabricated or deliberately manipulated information—for example, the intentional use of deepfakes to propagate political agenda on social media.	Mal-information is the deliberate abuse of private information with the intent to harm or intimidate. For example, a propagandist shares an opponent's mobile number (accurate information) with the intention for the person to be bombarded with malicious messages.

years to discredit opponents, influencing public opinion on political issues. In our study exploring disinformation campaigns during election periods in Malaysia and Indonesia (see Jalli and Idris, 2019), we spoke with several online propagandists from both countries. Political cybertroopers, employed by political parties in Malaysia and Indonesia, revealed that crafting false narratives with emotionally charged messages would elicit strong reactions from social media users on platforms like Facebook and Twitter. Four years later, during the most recent Malaysian general election in November 2022, similar disinformation campaigns were observed (Jalli, 2023). In this latest study on Malaysia's 15th general election, TikTok, which gained popularity during the COVID-19 outbreak in 2020, was heavily utilized by political actors and misinformed citizens to share emotive and inflammatory videos. Many of these videos contained contentious religious and racial messages. If left unaddressed, black propaganda can create misinformed citizens, potentially affecting political stability, and even national security.

And finally, the third color of propaganda is gray, where the information's origin is unclear, and the message's accuracy is questionable.

Lastly, gray propaganda is characterized by its unclear origin and the questionable accuracy of the message being disseminated. For instance, when browsing social media platforms like TikTok, you may come across videos praising political entities during the election period or Facebook pages excessively attacking certain political actors, leaving you wondering whether these pages are administered by propagandists or genuine individuals (see figure 1.1, for example). This uncertainty surrounding the legitimacy of the propaganda source and the authenticity of the message defines gray propaganda (Jowett and O'Donnell, 2018). The danger of gray propaganda lies in its ability to manipulate public opinion and undermine trust in legitimate sources of information, ultimately leading to confusion and division within society. See figure 1.2.

Figure 1.1 The Message on the Image Reads, "PH [Pakatan Harapan] supporters keep silent when Islam and ulama [religious clerics] are insulted. [But] when there are random rempit [Malaysia's slang and in this context rempit means uneducated] boys posted about May 13, PH supporters would say not to play with racial issues bla bla bla. Religion is a joke, right?" *Source:* Screenshot taken by Nuurianti Jalli. TikTok. November 22, 2022.

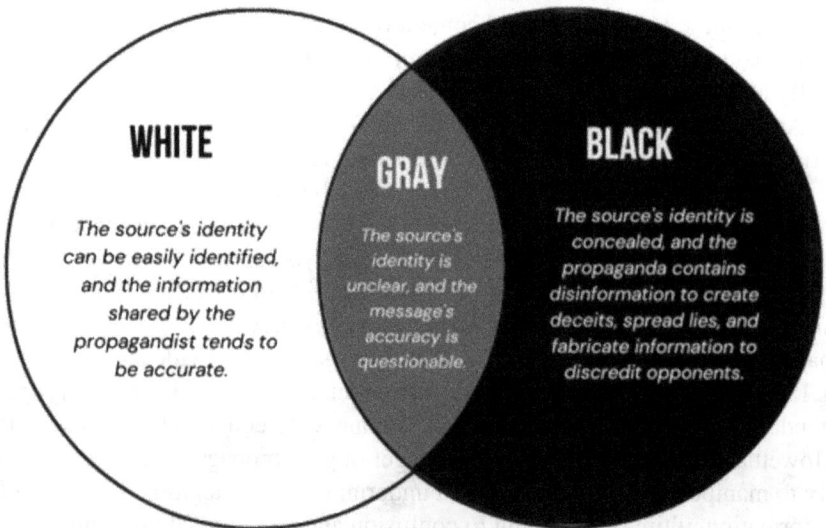

Figure 1.2 The Three Colors of Propaganda as Suggested by Jowett and O'Donnell (2018).

Rhetorical Triangle and Persuasive Propaganda

The efficacy of a propaganda campaign often hinges on the persuasiveness of the message being conveyed. Time and again, we have observed successful propaganda campaigns across the globe that employ compelling, persuasive messages shared repeatedly by their instigators. In this section, we will delve into the art of rhetoric to understand how well-crafted persuasive messages can alter the attitudes, values, beliefs, and behaviors of the target audience. This exploration will enable you to better assess the messages you encounter and comprehend why certain messages are more persuasive than others, why specific statements can evoke strong emotional reactions, and how effective propaganda can be skillfully constructed by utilizing the right words, gestures, and sentiments within the message.

Derived from the Greek language, rhetoric refers to the art of communicating effectively and persuasively to achieve specific objectives. Aristotle, the father of rhetoric, defined it as the faculty of observing the available means of persuasion in any given situation. By comprehending the appropriate appeals for crafting persuasive messages, propagandists can optimize the impact of their messages on their target audience. According to rhetorical principles, to create highly persuasive and influential messages, communicators (or propagandists, in the context of this book) must concentrate on three appeals, as identified by Aristotle: logos (logic), pathos (emotion), and ethos (credibility). To persuade others through any means of communication—from speech to text, and from images to visuals—one must craft their message by focusing on these three factors.

The premise is that people are more likely to be persuaded by someone who can present a logical argument (logos), which provides sound reasoning that enables the target audience to comprehend the message being conveyed. A message that resonates with the audience's emotions (pathos) captures their attention and engages them with the content being shared. Finally, establishing both the message and the communicator as credible (ethos) is crucial. Credibility can be achieved by presenting oneself as a person of good moral standing and convincing the audience of one's qualifications to share the message due to experience or educational background. Enhancing the message's credibility may involve providing supporting materials, ensuring the quality of the produced message, and other factors. See figure 1.3.

The three rhetorical appeals (logos, ethos, and pathos) are commonly employed to persuade an audience; however, their effectiveness can differ. Research has demonstrated that emotional appeals tend to be especially potent, as people are emotionally driven, and their emotions can influence their opinions and behaviors (Jerit, 2004; Crigler, 2007; Brader and George, 2013; Lamprianou and Antonis, 2019). In a 2004 study by Jerit, which

**ETHOS
(CREDIBILITY)**

The credibility of the
communicator and the
message being shared with the
audience.

**PATHOS
(EMOTION)**

Focusing on the emotional
appeal of the message.
Whether or not the
communicator's message can
strike the audience's
emotional chord.

**LOGOS
(LOGIC)**

The communicator's
ability to make a logical
argument in their
message to the audience.

**RHETORICAL
TRIANGLE**

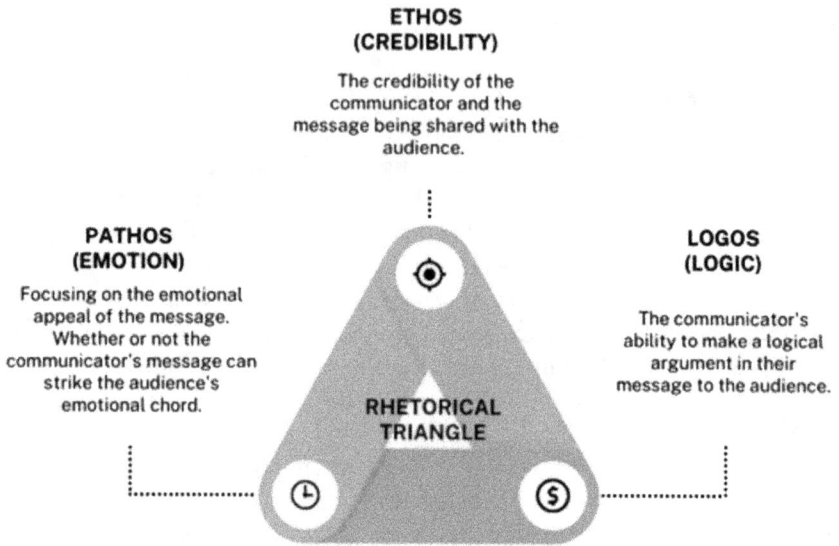

Figure 1.3 Aristotle's Rhetorical Triangle on Persuasive Message. *Source:* Chart by Nuurianti Jalli.

analyzed the rhetorical strategies utilized by political candidates during the 1988 Canadian federal election campaign, it was discovered that emotional appeals in political messages had a more enduring impact and were more prevalent in the rhetorical landscape compared to other types of appeals.

This assumption brings us to the next section in this chapter: psychology and propaganda.

Psychology and Propaganda

One way to comprehend propaganda is by understanding the impact of human psychology on information consumption. The notion that psychology plays a crucial role in propaganda is not new; in fact, it has been well documented in numerous studies dating back one hundred years (see Dodge, 1920; Doob and Robinson, 1934; Money-Kyrle, 1941). For instance, Money-Kyrle (1941) proposed that humans are not entirely rational and have always been susceptible to deception, as they tend to be credulous creatures. This means that even when presented with legitimate evidence and possessing the capacity to make sound judgments, humans can still fall victim to lies and manipulation. This vulnerability is particularly pronounced when exposed to emotionally charged propaganda, manipulated information that confirms personal biases (confirmation bias), and the influence of social environments, such as perceived majority opinions (in-group bias). As a result, even educated individuals can be irrational and believe in media propaganda.

Psychological research (Shepperd et al., 2008) has also found that humans tend to overestimate their cognitive abilities, exhibiting egotistical tendencies (Stephan et al., 1976), which often result in self-serving biases in decision-making. In the context of propaganda dissemination, this human trait leads us to believe that any information we perceive as "accurate" must be correct. The effects of self-serving bias have been observed worldwide in various situations, such as anti-vaccine propaganda during the COVID-19 pandemic. Despite numerous government campaigns advocating for vaccination, a significant number of anti-vaxxers refused to comply due to widespread anti-vaccine propaganda on social media (Wilson and Wisonge, 2020).

In-group bias: In-group bias is when people are inclined to believe information (in this case, lies) shared by what they perceive to be from their in-group.

Self-serving bias: Self-serving bias is when we evaluate ourselves more positively than others; therefore, we believe that the information we trust is the truth solely because we believe in it.

Confirmation bias: Confirmation bias is people's inclination to believe information aligned with their personal beliefs or hypotheses.

"It must be true; I saw it in print."

The perceived credibility of messages in mainstream media (such as those broadcasted via traditional outlets like TV, radio, and print press) among less educated communities is another factor contributing to a high susceptibility to propaganda. Money-Kyrle (1941) suggested in his essay that low literacy levels and perceived credibility of specific media platforms create opportunities for powerful entities (such as governments) to effectively shape public opinion. Controlling media, gatekeeping information, and selectively censoring content have been found to be some of the most effective propaganda tactics worldwide, particularly before the Internet era. Media control has aided many authoritarian governments in maintaining the status quo, as seen in Malaysia during the rule of Barisan Nasional from 1957 to 2008 (Jalli, 2013), Indonesia during the Suharto years (Gazali, 2002), and even during Hitler's propaganda campaign during World War II.

This has sparked interest in studies related to media effects, such as agenda-setting, where scholars explore the impact of mass media on human psychology and public opinion. For instance, the theory of agenda-setting in mass communication posits that the media "may not be successful much of the time in telling people what to think, but it is stunningly successful in telling people what to think about" (Cohen, 1963, pg. 13). This means that human

| Identify the target audience and conduct audience analysis | → | Identify the media channels to be used to propagate the agenda | → | Conduct a proper analysis on the select media channel | → | Repeatedly distribute the content on the select media to increase persuasive effect | The creation of 'media reality' **MEDIA AGENDA** |

Public perception of reality ← Issue becomes more salient — Repeatedly exposed to the propagated content

The creation of 'public reality'

PUBLIC AGENDA

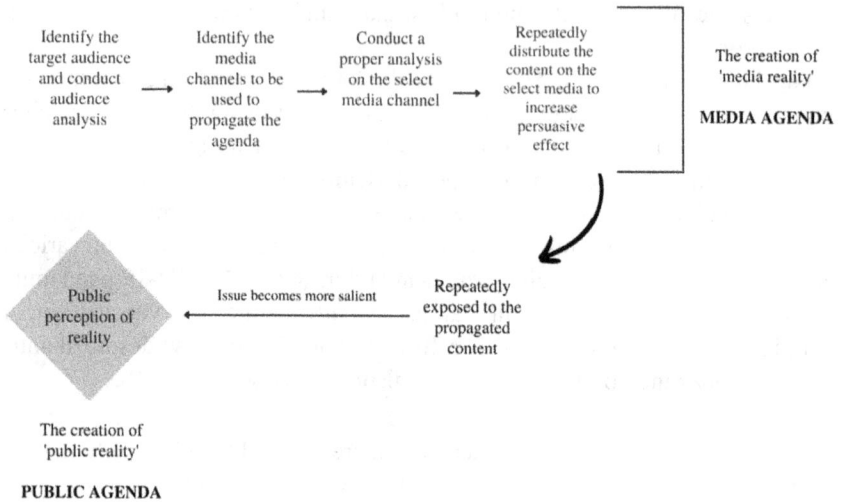

Figure 1.4   Agenda Setting and Propaganda Model: The Creation of Public Reality in the Media. This Model Was Developed Based on Hypotheses by Cohen (1963), McComb and Shaw (1972), and Jalli (2016). *Source:* Model by the authors.

minds can be influenced by the information they are exposed to. This notion has been supported by various studies, including one widely cited presidential election study conducted by Maxwell McCombs and Donald Shaw in 1968 (Weaver, Maxwell, and Shaw, 2004). Their research found that issues frequently appearing in the media influenced what was considered "important" in public discourse (McCombs and Shaw, 1972; Scheufele, 2000). In other words, they discovered that the issues emphasized by mass media, or the media agenda, are closely related to the topics discussed by the public, the public agenda. This finding establishes a strong association between the media agenda and the public agenda—the more an issue is highlighted by the media (media agenda), the more likely the issue is widely discussed in the public sphere (public agenda). Thus, if propagandists have a strong hold on mainstream media (in whatever form it takes in today's world), they have the advantage of shaping public discourse. See figure 1.4.

Propaganda Tactics

Numerous propaganda tactics have been employed to sway public opinion. In this section, we will explore common techniques used by instigators over the past decades and examine several new methods employed by influential politicians worldwide in recent years. We will begin by discussing the seven common propaganda tactics identified by the Institute for Propaganda

Analysis, and then proceed to analyze more recent techniques such as the "firehose of falsehood" propaganda model and other methods prevalent in Southeast Asia.

The Seven Common Tactics as Proposed by the Institute of Propaganda Analysis

The seven most prevalent strategies are frequently employed worldwide to evoke emotions and specific reactions from the public. Recognizing that propaganda is often seen as detrimental, especially in Western democracies, early propaganda theory suggested that raising public awareness of these tactics could help mitigate their impact on political realities (Baran and Davis, 2012). The Institute of Propaganda Analysis (IPA) was established in 1937 with the aim of helping scholars understand the effects of propaganda on public opinion, leading to the identification of these seven common methods (Baran and Davis Reisch, 2014). The US-based Institute for Propaganda Analysis (IPA) was founded in 1937 in response to growing concerns about the impact of propaganda on the public's critical thinking abilities. Active until 1942, the IPA's dissolution was due to dwindling support and insufficient funding (Skidmore, 2016). Key social scientists involved in its creation included Kirtley Mather, Edward A. Filene, and Clyde R. Miller, who gained support from numerous scholars, opinion leaders, educators, and journalists.

The first tactic is the bandwagon, and this propaganda method focuses on persuasive messages to influence the people to "follow the crowd" in supporting the propagandist. The bandwagon technique is usually carried out by portraying that the propagandist received a lot of support from the public, favored by the people. Therefore, it is the right decision to support them. The central message behind this is since "everybody is doing it," "everybody supports it," therefore, by supporting the propagandist, the people are on the "winning side." By playing the shared commonalities between the people, for example, in the context of Malaysia, racial and religious factors have a high tendency to attract the public bandwagon. Political entities and propagandists may use the paid crowd to publicize the propaganda. With the existence of the Internet, paid actors' orchestrated hypes are made easier, and the ability to create appealing and emotionally charged media content in today's world due to the presence of advanced media technologies makes propaganda, regardless of tactics, easier to spread.

The card stacking technique is where the propagandist uses parts of the information (facts) to strengthen his statements or arguments as proof to win support for himself, his beliefs, policies, and other matters. Through this technique, information may be presented out of context and key facts can be obscured by the propagandist to create political advantage. The propagandist lies by using overemphasis and under-emphasis methods, censorship, alteration, false testimony, and omitting facts to confuse and divert the masses. Card stacking makes half-truths as truths, unreal as real and vice-versa (AAUM, 1938).

The next technique is glittering generalities, when the propagandist uses "virtue words," "good words," "sugar-coated words," or "words filled with praise" to strengthen the positiveness of the propagandist's statements or arguments without offering supporting evidence. This technique is used to stir up and influence the emotions of the audience, consequently affecting followers to accept and approve the propagandist's statements or arguments without examining the evidence. Politicians often use this technique to inspire their audience (AAUM, 1938; Baran and Davis, 2012; Martin, 2018).

Another common propaganda tactic as suggested by IPA is name-calling. Unlike glittering generalities, name-calling techniques are employed by propagandists to label opponents using bad names, degrading labels, or negative remarks. This method is often used to create hate, fear, and doubts among the audience to generate negative perceptions against a certain subject that is to be perceived as incompetent, has no integrity, and cannot be trusted (AAUM, 1938). The objective of name-calling is to tarnish the image and reputation of the subject so that the audience will condemn and reject the subject. The name-calling technique can be applied directly or indirectly to the subject. This technique may be found in many forms including attacks on individuals, groups, policies, practices, and ideas (AAUM, 1938). It can also be in the form of single words, sentences, images (pictures or cartoons), or contexts in which the message is meant to ridicule the targeted subject.

Plain folk is a technique used by the propagandist to portray himself or herself as an ordinary person (thus plain folks), opposite of their actual status. Often this tactic is used to develop confidence among the targeted audience and create a sentiment that the propagandist is as "one of us" among the target audience. During elections, politicians will show their devotion to the people by being with them and living like them. The propagandist would use the plain folks' technique to win the hearts and minds of the people so that the propagandist's ideas will be perceived as "of the people" (AAUM, 1938; Baran and Davis, 2012).

The testimonial is a technique where the propagandist uses an ideal person (usually a respectable person or a person known by others) to endorse and promote the propagandist's ideas. The testimonial by that person does this well enough. This technique is considered as proof or evidence to the audience, thus strengthening the propagandist's ideas. Politicians use this technique to show that they are worthy of the people's support and votes. Due to its motive to influence others to agree with the propagandist's ideas, the testimonial technique could also be used as part of the bandwagon technique (Baran and Davis, 2012; Martin, 2018).

The transfer is a technique whereby the propagandist associates himself or herself with other subjects or entities that wield authority and respect from others so that the targeted audience would accept the propagandist's ideas, policies, or programs. Symbols, as they stir emotions, are frequently used in the transfer technique. The transfer technique is used to portray the authority as supporting and approving the propagandist in terms of ideas, policies, programs, or other matters, and the same is expected from the targeted audience (AAUM, 1938; Baran and Davis, 2012; Martin, 2018). See table 1.3 and figure 1.5.

The Russian's "Firehose of Falsehood" Propaganda Model

The notorious "firehose of falsehood" model, often attributed to Russia's propaganda approach, is a highly sophisticated technique that involves overwhelming the target audience with a torrent of lies and false stories, more than they can possibly keep up with. This tactic creates significant challenges for fact-checkers, who often struggle to process the sheer volume of information due to the limited number of human content moderators and the limitations of artificial intelligence (AI) technology. AI often falls short in tracing content posted in non-mainstream languages, including indigenous languages, dialects, and slang.

This same issue is also prevalent in Southeast Asia, where fact-checking agencies are in their infancy in many countries, and the region is home to over 1,000 languages and dialects. Internet content in these languages creates a systemic problem for identifying and verifying information, even with human content moderators. Propagandists may exploit this loophole by targeting specific communities with content in indigenous languages and dialects, bypassing the "fact-checking barriers" established by fact-checking organizations.

Consequently, the final defense against propaganda in indigenous languages or dialects rests with the people, who can participate in fact-checking initiatives by reporting suspicious content on social media. Previous research on fact-checking challenges in Southeast Asia found that agencies such as MAFINDO in Indonesia and VERAFiles in the Philippines face difficulties monitoring disinformation, misinformation, and mal-information online due to the limited number of human fact-checkers, who are generally more effective than non-human fact-checking technologies (Jalli, 2020). See table 1.2.

The term "firehose of falsehood" was first introduced by Christopher Paul and Mirian Matthews (2016), who tried to highlight the similarity of Putin's

Table 1.3   The Seven Common Propaganda Tactics as Identified by the Institute of Propaganda Analysis (IPA)

	Tactics	Definitions	Examples
1	Bandwagon	A propaganda technique used by propagandists to make the target audience to "contribute to their cause and follow the crowd."	"Everyone believes that this policy will benefit the community, you should support this effort to create a better nation for everyone."
2	Card stacking	A tactic used by propagandists to present a selected part of the story that is twisted or uses a false logical argument to construct a persuasive idea, program, persona, or product.	"Looking at the implementation of increased taxes (*truth*) recently by the ruling government, it has resulted price hikes in the marketplace (*distorted* fact)." In a study on South China Sea disputes between Indonesia and China, research done by Wijaya (2018) found that Indonesian news outlets such as Kompas and ANTARA used card-stacking techniques in framing news relating to the dispute and Indonesia-China bilateral diplomatic relations. Common news framing on the issue is that the ongoing South China disputes should not affect Indonesia-China relations and could be solved through diplomatic dialogues.
3	Glittering generalities	When propagandists use impressive and eloquent words in showing the "virtue" of an idea, people, or organization to create public acceptance and amazement.	"Our nation is a democratic country; we appreciate feedback from the public on how we can move forward with creating a better nation."
4	Name-calling	When propagandists give a bad name for an idea, people, or organization and create hatred toward the object.	"Leaders of the opposition party are communist sympathizers, and corrupt!"
5	Plain folks	When propagandists justify their ideas in the name "of the people" or "plain folks."	"I am doing this for the people of the nation. As a representative of the people, as a citizen of this country, it is my responsibility to pursue this cause for you on your behalf, on our behalf."

| 6 | Testimonials | When propagandists strategically use prominent and important individuals to give testimonials or support their ideas. | Using social media influencers to support government policies. The propagandist hopes that your feelings about the famous person will transfer to the product or cause he or she endorses. However, it is important to note that not all testimonials are propaganda. Arab-Israeli social media influencer and travel blogger Nusier Yassin (Nas Daily) was reportedly paid by the Israeli government to propagate pro-Israel propaganda, including in his social media postings (Nassar and Abunimah, 2020). The call for a boycott of Nusier Yassin by pro-Palestinian supporters, including the Muslims in Malaysia and Indonesia, resulted in him being barred from entering both countries (Barreiro, 2021). |
| 7 | Transfer | When propagandists associate themselves with other authoritative or respectable entities so that target audience would accept the propagated ideas. Transfer can also be done via a symbolic manner. | "Similar policy is implemented in other countries and is widely supported by world leaders like President Biden of the United States, and President Justin Trudeau of Canada." *Symbolic:* When politicians give speeches behind a country's flag as a sign of patriotism and loyalty to the country. Such use of symbols only becomes propaganda when it is strategically orchestrated to create an emotional message. |

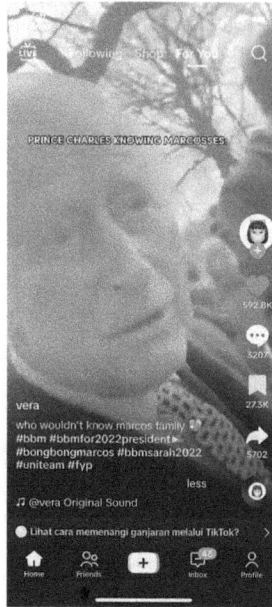

Figure 1.5 Example of the Use of Transfer Technique during the 2022 Philippines General Election on TikTok. A Pro-Ferdinand Romualdez (BongBong) Marcos Jr., @vera (Changed Their TikTok Handle to @ikrnc0le after the Election), Uploaded a Video with Prince Charles "allegedly" Knowing the Marcos Family. The Video Also Contained a Picture of the British Prince with Mrs. Imelda Marcos (Mother of BongBong Marcos, Former 10th First Lady of the Philippines) to Attract Voters Ahead of the Election. The Video Received 447.4 Thousand Likes and 2.6 Million Views as of June 1, 2022. *Source:* Screenshot taken by Nuurianti Jalli. November 22, 2022.

propaganda-spreading strategy when annexing Crimea and Georgia into Russia with the propaganda tactic used by Trump during the US presidential election campaign in 2016.

Some distinctive features of the "firehose of falsehood" propaganda model include:

1. High volume of information.
2. Information/propaganda is shared via multiple channels. (People tend to believe in information shared via multiple sources. The central hypothesis here is the more channels you share the "falsehood", the more credible it will seem).
3. Rapid, continuous, and repetitive.
4. Make no commitment to reality.
5. Make no commitment to consistency.

The most intriguing aspect of this propaganda model is that the false information created by propagandists doesn't have to be believable and can even be blatant lies. Various researchers support this notion, finding that lies don't necessarily need to be believable to be effective [see Little (2018) and Christopher and Miriam (2019)]. Such false information can significantly influence public opinion. World leaders like Vladimir Putin and Donald Trump have benefited from using this technique in their political campaigns, garnering substantial public support. In Indonesia, President Joko Widodo was also accused of employing the same approach during the 2019 general election, contaminating the Indonesian digital space through the use of buzzers and misinformed supporters, ultimately resulting in his victory that year (Jalli and Idris, 2019; Haqqi, 2020; Medistiara, 2021). A few potential reasons why using blatant lies may work in propaganda campaigns include low education levels (Idris, 2019), intergroup biases, self-serving biases, and confirmation biases (Brennan, 2017; Cole, 2022; Jalli, 2020).

Other Propaganda Techniques

This final section will examine various additional propaganda techniques that have been used to manipulate public perception and create fear, discord, and anxiety around the world and in Southeast Asia. These techniques include panic mongering, creating confusion, using populist rhetoric, scapegoating, character assassination, rewriting history, false dilemma, whataboutism, astroturfing, red-herring, and poisoning the well.

Panic mongering is a propaganda technique that involves spreading fear and alarm about a particular issue or event to manipulate public opinion or gain political or financial advantage. This technique often uses sensationalist language and imagery, and it can be used to create a sense of urgency or crisis, often with the goal of getting people to take a certain action, such as supporting a particular policy or candidate. Panic mongering can be used to create fear around issues such as crime, terrorism, public health, and the economy, and it can be used to justify certain actions, such as increasing government surveillance or spending on defense. It can also be used to create a sense of urgency and demand for a particular product or service. This was evident during the COVID-19 pandemic when anti-Chinese propaganda spread online, leading to increased hate toward Asians, particularly of East Asian descent, in the United States and other countries (Gover, Shannon, and Langton, 2020). This same pattern was found in Malaysia and Indonesia, resulting in increased stigmatization toward Mainland Chinese at the beginning of the COVID-19 outbreak (Idris et al., 2022; Idris and Jalli, 2020).

Next is *confusion* or "muddying the waters" propaganda method, which can be understood as a technique to create confusion and uncertainty about a particular issue or event, usually with the goal of deflecting criticism or avoiding accountability. This technique often involves presenting a large amount of conflicting or misleading information, making it difficult for people to determine the truth. It can be used to create doubt about the credibility of legitimate sources of information or to obscure the facts of a situation. By muddying the waters, propagandists can create a sense of ambiguity or complexity around a particular issue making it more difficult for people to form an opinion or to take action. It can also be used to present a false narrative or alternative facts to mislead people on a particular topic. This technique was observed during the 2021 military coup in Myanmar, where pro-military supporters and soldiers uploaded disinformation on Facebook and TikTok to confuse and misinform anti-coup protestors (Peter, Fishbein, and Nunu, 2021). In Southeast Asia, like in many other parts of the world, propagandists often use disinformation to "muddy the waters" with the aim of gaining political advantage.

The third technique is *populism* propaganda, which often uses a rhetoric that is appealing to the common people. Propagandists strategically create narratives emphasizing their frustrations and anger toward the establishment (the elites in society) and portraying the propagandist as the only one who truly understands and represents the will of the people. This technique often uses simple, emotive language and imagery, and it often taps into issues such as immigration, economic inequality, and political corruption. Populist propaganda can be used by politicians, political parties, and other groups to mobilize support and gain power, but it can also be used to sow division and undermine democratic institutions. These techniques can be easily found in multiple countries in Southeast Asia, such as in Malaysia, where populism is often used by government critics to influence public opinion toward political elites, which includes the royal families and high-ranking government officials, through social media campaigns (Khoo, 2018) or utilized by the government's number one, such as former president Duterte "Dutertismo" political style to appeal to the masses (Capuno, 2020). In the Philippines for example, former president Rodrigo Duterte successfully won the 2016 presidential election by tapping into Filipinos' deep frustration with decades of poverty. Duterte methodically used social media to spread his populist propaganda by framing the issue of the status quo in the Philippines as the fault of the "elites" (*dilawan*, Liberal party, his political opponent). Repeatedly appealing to the public through strategic disinformation campaigns with populist undertones, Duterte was able to connect with Filipino identities (Kho, 2019). See figure 1.6.

Figure 1.6 Political Activist and Graphic Designer Fahmi Reza Launched a Digital NFT Artwork Titled *Monyet Istana* (Castle's Monkey) in April 2022 as a Symbolic Act of Protest against the Malaysian Government for Continuously Abusing the Sedition Act 1948, and Section 233 of Communication and Multimedia Act 1998, as a Political Tool to Silence Satire, Dissent, Criticism toward Political Elites Including the Monarchy and Royal Families. Fahmi Reza, as Observed by Some Scholars, Had Adopted the Populist Approach, and Over the Years Has Played the Same Sentiment across His Social Media Postings. *Source:* Screenshot from the authors. Sourced from Facebook.

Scapegoating, also known as "othering," is a propaganda technique that involves blaming a certain group or individual for a problem or issue, often as a way to avoid taking responsibility or to redirect attention away from the real causes of the problem. This technique often targets marginalized or minority groups, and it can be used to create division, hatred, and fear toward that group. Scapegoating can be used by political leaders, media outlets, or other groups to deflect criticism, shift blame, or mobilize support for their policies or agenda. It can also be used to justify discriminatory or violent actions against the targeted group, creating a sense of moral superiority among the scapegoater's supporters. This technique is often observed in the Southeast Asian region, as seen in the coverage of the Indonesia-Chinese disputes in the South China Sea, where Chinese media such as Xinhua, *China Daily*, and *People's Daily* have overtly placed blame on Indonesia's policies, including blaming Indonesia for allegedly attacking a Chinese fishing vessel while it was carrying out normal fishing operations on permitted fishing grounds (Wijaya, 2018).

Character assassination is a propaganda technique that aims to tarnish the reputation of an individual or group in order to undermine their credibility and influence. This can be done through spreading false information or rumors, manipulating, selectively editing quotes or statements, or using innuendo or insinuation. Other tactics include the use of social media or paid individuals to spread false information about the target. The goal is to create a negative perception of the target in the eyes of the public, making it difficult for them to be successful in their endeavors or be taken seriously. An example of this is seen in Malaysia where the incumbent Prime Minister, Anwar Ibrahim, had his character attacked during his political crisis with former Prime Minister Mahathir Mohammad in the 1990s. He was accused of sexual misconduct and corruption which led him to be sacked from his position (Abbott, 2001).

Another interesting propaganda technique observed in Southeast Asia is which often involves altering or distorting historical facts or events to influence public opinion or to support a particular agenda. This method often used to create a new narrative or version of history that supports the views of the propagandist or undermines the views of their opponents. It can be used to create a sense of national pride or to justify certain actions or policies. "Rewriting history" can be done through a variety of means, including altering or suppressing historical records, distorting or exaggerating historical events, and promoting a particular interpretation of history. It can also be done through other means, such as rewriting history textbooks, monuments, statues, street names, holidays, and other symbols that represent history. The goal of rewriting history is to shape people's understanding of the past and influence their views on the present and the future. For instance, in the 2022 Philippines General Election, President Ferdinand Romualdez (BongBong) Marcos was heavily criticized for recreating new narratives surrounding his family's history, the controversial Marcos family, through networked propaganda campaigns on social media like Facebook and TikTok (Symons-Brown and Henry, 2022; Pierson, 2022). His father, Ferdinand Marcos, who was the former president of the country from 1965 to 1986, was famous for his controversial leadership and his regime was marked by authoritarianism, corruption, human rights abuses, and suppression of political opposition. During his presidency, Ferdinand Marcos implemented policies that led to widespread poverty and economic inequality, while he and his family became extremely wealthy. He also implemented martial law in 1972, which gave him dictatorial powers and suppressed civil liberties. But through his son, BongBong Marcos' strategic social media campaigns, his political sins were diluted down through aggressive online campaigns.

False dilemma, also known as false dichotomy or the either-or fallacy, is a propaganda technique that involves presenting two options or alternatives as the only possible options when, in actuality, other options are available. This technique is often used by propagandists to simplify complex issues and present them in a way that is easy to understand and can be used to manipulate public opinion or force people to make a decision based on limited information. False dilemma can be used to create a sense of urgency or crisis, to force people to choose between two options that are both undesirable and to create a false sense of choice. This technique can be used in different forms, such as presenting a false choice between two candidates, two policies, two sides of a conflict, or two alternatives. The goal is to limit the range of options available and present a false choice as the only one, making it more likely that the target audience will make a decision that aligns with the views of the propagandist. An example of false dilemma in political campaign is when a candidate presents a false choice to voters, suggesting that they can either vote for the candidate or vote for chaos and destruction. This presents the election as a binary choice between a positive outcome (the candidate winning) and a negative outcome (chaos and destruction), with no other alternatives being presented. This creates a sense of urgency and pressure on voters to choose the candidate in order to avoid the negative outcome, while in reality, other available candidates are not being presented as viable alternatives, thereby making the choice not binary but multi-dimensional.

The next technique is *whataboutism*, and this propaganda method involves the act of strategically deflecting criticism or avoiding accountability by redirecting attention to an unrelated issue or action, often by asking "what about" some other person or group. The goal of this technique is to change the subject, shift the blame, or create a false equivalence between the two issues, rather than address the original criticism or accusation. It is often used to avoid taking responsibility for one's own actions or to discredit the opposing side by pointing out their own flaws or misdeeds. This technique can be used in different forms such as, "what about when the other side did this?" or "what about the event that happened before?" It can also be used to create a false balance by claiming that both sides are equally guilty of some wrongdoing, thus discounting political sins. By using this tactic, the propagandist aims to create confusion, avoid accountability, and deflect criticism by redirecting the attention to something else. For example, at the height of the 1MDB scandal involving the former prime minister Najib Razak of Malaysia, he deflected media attention toward his case to rising national debt in 2022 to the two administrations that came after him. He claimed that Malaysia's overall debt had risen for over RM300 million after his leadership was toppled down and the new administration took over ("Najib blames Dr. M," 2022).

Astroturfing is a propaganda method that involves creating the appearance of a grassroots movement or popular support for a particular issue or product when in reality, it is being orchestrated by a small group of individuals or organizations. This can be done through various means, such as creating fake social media accounts or websites, paying people to participate in rallies or protests, or creating fake letters to the editor or online comments that appear to be from ordinary citizens. The goal of astroturfing is essentially to create the illusion of widespread public support for a particular issue or product when, in reality, it is being driven by a small group of individuals or organizations with a specific agenda. Astroturfing is widely popular in Malaysia and Indonesia as one of the key methods to influence public opinion, particularly during election seasons (Jalli and Idris, 2019), as it has been proven effective in influencing public opinion, swaying political decisions, and creating a false sense of consensus.

Another tactic worth mentioning is *red-herring,* where propagandists introduce irrelevant or misleading information or arguments in order to divert attention away from the real issue or to distract from a critical line of inquiry. This technique can be used to create confusion, to shift the focus of a conversation, to avoid answering a question, or to make an opponent's argument appear weak. The term "red herring" comes from the practice of training hunting dogs by dragging a strong-smelling fish, such as a red herring, across a scent trail with the aim of distracting the dog and changing its focus. Similarly, in propaganda, a red herring is used to mislead or distract the audience and divert their attention away from the main point. It can be used to introduce irrelevant information or to present a false argument to change the focus of the conversation. One instance of red herring propaganda in Malaysia is when, in the past, former Najib Razak's administration had used the issue of national security to deflect criticism and avoid accountability for 1MDB corruption scandals. When Najib Razak was facing criticism for mismanagement of public funds, his administration would often redirect the conversation by claiming that any criticism was a threat to national security and undermined the stability of Malaysia. By introducing the idea of national security, Najib Razak's government was able to shift the focus of the conversation away from the original issue of corruption and onto a different topic, diluting public attention toward the massive 1MDB scandal.

And finally, the *poisoning the well* propaganda tactic involves preemptively discrediting a person or group to undermine their credibility or to make their arguments less effective. This technique can be used to discredit an individual or group before they have the opportunity to speak or to make their arguments by spreading false information or rumors or by presenting them in a negative light. The goal is to create a negative perception of the person or group so that the audience will not take their arguments or statements seriously. This technique can be used in different forms, such as personal attacks, character assassination, or spreading false rumors. It can also be used to create a negative perception of a person or group by associating them with something negative or undesirable. The name "poisoning the well" comes from the idea of contaminating a water source before someone has a chance to drink from it. In the same way, an individual or group is discredited before they can present their arguments. See textbox 1.1.

TEXTBOX 1.1

Grace Natalie of the Indonesia Solidarity Party's character assassination disinformation campaign by "Hulk" @hulk_ind.

Grace Natalie, the founder of the Indonesian Solidarity Party (PSI), was a young female Chinese Christian politician in President Joko (Jokowi) Widodo's coalition during the Indonesia's 2019 elections. As she gained popularity among young voters during the campaign period, Grace was hit by a malicious rumor spread by a Twitter account named "Hulk" (@hulk_ind), which rumored that Grace had a sexual relationship with Jakarta's former governor, Basuki Tjhaja Purnama (Ahok) (Purnamasari, 2018). Ahok, a controversial political figure in Indonesia, was embroiled in a political controversy for allegedly blaspheming against Islam (Osman and Waikar, 2018). The salicious rumor gained traction quickly after it was covered by gossip sites and reported to the public as "breaking news", revealing information that wasn't known to the public and claiming it to be true. Grace, a former journalist, purportedly jumped into politics with the help of Ahok after interviewing him for an assignment. The encounter later bloomed into a romantic relationship. Hulk, through their Twitter account, claimed that they had a copy of the "couple" sex video and would release the video to the public when the time was right. With low media and information literacy in Indonesia (Harsono, 2022), the propaganda campaign initiated by Hulk, potentially a professional buzzer, spread like wildfire. The deliberately engineered salacious rumor to assassinate Grace Natalie's good character worked effectively as Grace started to lose followers and support at the height of the controversy.

CHAPTER SUMMARY

In this chapter, we explored propaganda as a form of manipulative communication that has been employed throughout history to influence people's opinions and behaviors. Propaganda is often linked to political or ideological messages and can manifest in various forms, such as written or spoken language, images, or symbols, as demonstrated through multiple case studies in this chapter. There are several types of propaganda pervasive in today's society: white propaganda presents information in a straightforward manner and is likely to be accurate; gray propaganda has an unclear origin, and the accuracy of the message is questionable; and black propaganda disseminates false or misleading information. Propaganda can be detrimental to democracy by disseminating disinformation or misleading content to the public, leading to the spread of misinformation and the manipulation of public opinion. This is particularly hazardous in a democratic society, where citizens are expected to make informed decisions based on accurate information.

The chapter also delved into various propaganda techniques, including the seven common tactics identified by the Institute for Propaganda Analysis (IPA) and more recent methods like the "firehose of falsehood" propaganda model. These techniques have been adapted and employed by political leaders and organizations around the world, demonstrating the continued relevance and effectiveness of propaganda in shaping public opinion. Furthermore, the chapter examined the relationship between psychology and propaganda, highlighting how human cognitive biases and emotions can make individuals susceptible to propaganda. By understanding these psychological factors and becoming aware of the common tactics used in propaganda, people can better protect themselves from being manipulated and make more informed decisions in a democratic society. In conclusion, propaganda remains a potent tool for influencing public opinion and behavior. As society evolves and communication technology advances, new methods of propaganda will undoubtedly emerge. It is essential for citizens to remain vigilant, recognize propaganda techniques, and strive to make informed decisions based on accurate information to ensure the health and longevity of democracy.

Chapter 2

Propaganda in the Digital Era

This chapter delves into the use of propaganda in the digital age, which has been utilized by various entities such as governments, political parties, and organizations to sway public opinion and shape societal norms. With the advent of digital technologies, propaganda has taken on new forms and has become a prevalent force on the Internet. The chapter examines the recent trends and definitions of propaganda in the digital era, including how it has adapted to the progress in communication and information technologies. It also investigates the strategies that are frequently employed in the digital space, including message-based and distribution-based techniques, and how digital media features can make propaganda messages more complex.

PROPAGANDA ON SOCIAL MEDIA

Gofar Hilman, an Indonesian radio broadcaster with more than 850 thousand followers on Instagram and 1.2 million subscribers on his YouTube channel, once posted a short video on Instagram that he later regretted and apologized to his followers. In a video he posted on Instagram, Hilman, the 38-year-old man who once broke the national record for longest radio broadcasts, encouraged his followers to focus on themselves and be innovative during the pandemic, and he stated that it was not fair to blame anyone for people's unemployment during the time of a global health crisis. Using his platform, Hilman also emphasized the need for the younger generation to find creative ways to create jobs, as everyone needs employment during the global health crisis. In mid-2020, Hilman joined forces with other prominent Indonesian celebrities and social media influencers to promote this message using the hashtag #IndonesiaButuhKerja (Indonesia needs jobs).

The hashtag #IndonesiaButuhKerja was later found to be a part of a social media campaign by the Indonesian government in support of the Omnibus Law, a controversial job creation bill (Adjie, 2020). This bill has faced criticism from academics, labor unions, NGOs, and university students for its potential negative impacts on the country's natural resources, environment, human rights, and workers (Mulyanto, 2020). During the pandemic, thousands of protesters across Indonesia took to the streets for three days to oppose the bill. Subsequently, many of these protesters were arrested by the police (BBC, 2020). Hilman and other social media influencers involved in the campaign posted public apologies and dissociated themselves from the government's political campaign. Some of them, including Hilman and a rising Indonesian musician Ardhito Pramono, admitted that they did not check where the money came from and returned the payment. As a reaction to that social media campaign, the presidential staff, led by Donny Adian, denied that President Joko Widodo's (Jokowi) office ordered the campaign. Despite the public's strong reaction to the incident, Adian did not see social media influencers' support of the controversial bill as a problem (Adjie, 2020).

In the era of social media, using celebrities and micro-influencers is a common strategy employed by governments to shape a favorable public opinion toward public policy (Neyazi, 2019; Idris, 2019). Social media is used for networking, updating information, and as a key platform for marketing, advocacy, establishing socio-political movements, and spreading ideas. Using social media, influencers have been one of the main strategies employed by the Indonesian government in promoting public policy and government programs, as well as dominating online public discussion. This strategy can be seen in Indonesian government programs, such as promoting public vaccination for COVID-19 (Bernie and Syambudi, 2021), health protocols (Tambun, 2020), and a tourism recovery program at the beginning of the COVID-19 pandemic in Indonesia, which was allocated a budget of USD 4.9 million (CNN Indonesia, 2020). The same strategy was also applied during the revision of the anti-corruption law or KPK Law and the selection of commissioners for the Corruption Eradication Commission (Adyatama and Wibowo, 2020).

In the case of promoting the Omnibus Law, no one has taken responsibility for coordinating and managing the twenty celebrities who were used to promote the hashtag. Even mass media did not continue to follow the story and stopped publishing it. The most common characteristics of propaganda in the digital era are sudden virality, untraceable sources, disinformation, and deceitful coordinated messages, such as in the case of the support for the job creation bill.

Definition: Recap

As discussed in chapter 1, propaganda has a long history as a strategy for public persuasion. The term itself has a neutral meaning—to promote or spread information—but it has come to have a negative connotation when associated with public political persuasion. Nowadays, propagandists—government, corporate, political actors, or terrorist organizations—generally use the Internet and other information technologies as their tools for spreading their version of information that traditional journalism may not buy into (Kovach and Rosentiel, 2014). Websites and social media have become places for propagandists to counter information and criticism from mass media. At times, they are also sources of information for journalists. However, if journalists fail to verify the information, websites and social media can become the perfect medium for propagandists to disseminate deceitful messages. A trending political conversation can encourage mass media organizations to produce and publish articles based on the topic, relying only on controversial tweets or posts on social media by politicians. Even though the tweets or posts are sent from official accounts, publishing them to attract readers can involve the news organization in spreading unverified information.

The new media characteristics of interactivity, multimedia, and connectedness make the propaganda process different from that of the past, when communication tended to be one-way through mass media. Social media networks can increase the number of channels to disseminate messages at a lower cost. Interactivity, represented by the "comment" feature, provides more space for propaganda messages, as they are not only in the original post but also in the discussion in the "comments" section. In fact, the foundation of social media algorithms is designed to promote interactions. On social media, some posts may appear "neutral," for example, a person sharing the updated number of victims in the Paris attacks in 2015. However, the comments written by friends in the comments section cannot be separated from the post and can be interpreted as part of the news by readers. The multimedia characteristic provides more space for visuals, and less for written messages, thus creating opportunities for propaganda strategies such as name-calling and glittering generalities.

On social media platforms like Twitter the space for a message is limited to 280 characters, which prompts people to send more eye-catching and concise messages to attract attention. In the early days of Twitter in Indonesia, many anonymous social media accounts were created to post a series of tweets that attacked government officials, politicians, political parties, and presidential candidates (Hamid, 2014; Masduki, 2022). Two of the most popular accounts, such as @triomacan2000 and @kurawa, had hundreds of thousands of followers who effectively engaged with propaganda messages through the Twitter comment feature. The strategy they used was to post seemingly scandalous or corrupt stories and attack the reputations of the politicians or officials involved. Their followers would fuel the conversation by posting opinions, memes, and additional information in the comments.

In the digital era, particularly with the widespread use of smartphones, propaganda messages can reach people easily through social media and more private spheres, such as group chats in messaging applications or small interest groups in online forums. In her book "Private Sphere," Papacharissi (2010) explains that the private space facilitated by the Internet allows individuals to produce and distribute their own messages or selectively consume information based on personal preferences or identity. At the same time, people can also choose to disengage from certain social networks or information they do not want to receive. Communication technology allows us to switch between active and inactive modes while engaging with public issues. In other words, the Internet enables new forms of political participation in the private sphere that also connects to the public sphere. Like other types of information such as education, campaigns, or news, propaganda messages can enter our private sphere and engage with us at any time, even within a small circle of social networks we have selected.

Examples of new private space that turns into political deliberation and participation can be seen in how Indonesian youth utilize the video-based app TikTok to promote their local identities and advocate issues in their regions. As a country that consists of around 1,300 ethnicities (Statistics Indonesia, 2015), it is hard to find room to express, celebrate, and negotiate local identities in a public space without worrying that it will threaten the national identity. The New Order regime often hindered regional expressions because it was feared that it would reduce the strength of the Indonesian identity. At that time, the regime considered Indonesian identity to be formed from the best elements or the peaks of regional cultures (Idris and Gismar, 2021). As a result, regionalism is not expressed as much as it should be, but through the boundaries set by the government, while local culture is left to be displayed only through songs, dances, and traditional clothes. Video-based social media platforms such as TikTok can offer an alternative close space for local Indonesian youth to express their local identities through songs, videos, and hashtags such as #jawapride, #kalimantanpride, #papuapride, #sumaterapride, #sulawesipride, #minangpride, #batakpride, or #bugispride (Idris and Gismar, 2021). Compared to other youth in Indonesia, the personal expression of identity is even harder for Papuan youth in the easternmost part of Indonesia because of the long political conflict and pro-independence movement on the island (Bakhshi, 2021). On TikTok, videos with the hashtag #papuaparide not only contained dances, selfies, or customs about the ethnic groups but also contained political statements to counter negative stereotypes about the tribe or region, pride in local identity, and local problems in the community, such as discrimination and the exploitation of Papua mines (Idris and Gismar, 2021).

Moreover, with the same hashtag that shows songs and dances from Papuans, the platforms also show many videos containing messages advocating for the freedom of Papua from Indonesia, as well as videos from the Indonesian national army to promote the opposite. The availability of such platforms opens more room for propaganda messages to enter larger audiences within their personal spaces, which the Indonesian government or other social systems could not interrupt (Jalli, 2022). The direct connection between the private and public spheres, mediated by digital platforms and the Internet, could push propaganda messages from the public sphere to an intimate space where messages are internalized among members of the groups (Asmolov, 2019). To some extent, those private spaces will also be a fertile ground for conspiracy theories (Johns and Cheong, 2021).

Modern propaganda utilizes interactive multimedia and technology to spread disinformation through social media platforms. Engagement on these platforms, including reach, impressions, reactions, sharing, and comments, can influence the virality of a post. Any form of engagement—from viewership such as reach and impression, passive engagement such as leaving "like" and "reactions," active engagements such as sharing and comments—can determine whether a post can go viral. The contribution of any form of engagement to content virality creates strategies to make a post go viral, such as using the social media army or also known as "buzzer" to amplify messages (Jalli and Idris, 2019), using clickbait titles to generate readers, and using computational programs or bots to launch and amplify messages. In other words, online public discussion has been manipulated by a handful of sources, including those that are driven by algorithms (Neyazi, 2019). A study on computational propaganda by Bradshaw and Howard (2017) at the University of Oxford shows that bots were found to spread fake news in many countries, including in Southeast Asia, such as the Philippines and Vietnam.

In Indonesia, bots have been used by news organizations to promote their agenda on social media and increase readership (Fahmi, 2019), as well as by government agencies to support unpopular policies, such as the palm oil industry. In 2018, the European Union voted to phase out palm oil from its Renewable Energy Directive, which hurt Indonesia's palm oil exports to the EU and the country's economy, as it is the largest palm oil producer in the world. Palm oil industry in Indonesia contributed $12 billion to the national economy in 2017 (Normala, 2018).

In response, the Indonesian government launched a campaign called "Sawit Baik" in 2019 to promote the benefits of palm oil and counter the negative information about the industry. However, the campaign faced public backlash due to a forest fire in one of the country's largest palm oil plantations and criticism from pressure groups. A social network analysis showed that the campaign was primarily supported by bots and failed to gain traction due to a lack of support from other propaganda machines. The account associated with the campaign is now suspended by Twitter. In general, bots can be used to initiate propaganda messages and amplify them, but without support from other propaganda tools such as social media influencers and troops, their ability to influence public opinion is limited.

To support Indonesia's negotiation with the EU, in 2019, the Indonesian Ministry of Communication and Information (Kominfo) launched a campaign named "Sawit Baik" (Good Palm Oil) in 2019 to promote the benefits of palm oil and counter the negative information about the industry (Sindonews, 2019). Kominfo called the launching event of the campaign an influencer meeting, where they invited social media influencers to attend. At the event, one of the speakers, a legislative member of Indonesia, asked for public support to fight the negative campaign toward Indonesia's palm oil industry, as they believed the EU's restrictions were influenced by the opinion war on social media (Nurfaizah, 2019). The campaign turned out to get public backlash because, at the same time, a forest fire occurred in Riau, one of the largest palm oil plantations in Indonesia (Greenpeace, 2019). According to Munggaran (2019), a social network analysis of the #SawitBaik conversation showed that the positive conversation was mainly sent out by an official account of an oil palm plantation fund management (Badan Pengelola Dana Perkebunan Kepala Sawit) @bpdp_sawit. The same conversation was then being promoted by @SawitBaikID—an official account for the campaign established by Kominfo but amplified by newly created Twitter accounts that only had one or two followers. Besides, the cluster of conversations was excluded from the main conversation related to criticism of the palm oil industry and government campaigns. The @bpdp_sawit did not even engage in or try to counter the public criticism and was mainly broadcasting messages. In other words, the campaign was supported mainly by bots and failed to propagate the issue due to public backlash caused by a forest fire in one of the country's largest palm oil plantations and criticism from pressure groups.

Later, Kominfo's minister, Rudiantara, stated that he was not aware of such a campaign supported by his ministry (Kurnia, 2019). Today, the account @bpdp_sawit is suspended by Twitter, and @SawitBaikID is inactive. In most cases, bots can often be used to launch propaganda messages and spread them widely by amplifying them through a larger network of conversations, making them viral. However, without support from other propaganda tools such as social media influencers and teams, their ability to influence public discussions and people's opinions is limited.

Participatory Propaganda

The old definition of propaganda that centralized on an organization's top-down communication strategy is no longer suitable in the digital era. Studies on the US presidential election show that propaganda could also initiate and trigger the audience, where they were actively producing deceitful messages, spreading disinformation, and forming communities of the same ideologies (so-called filter bubble) that later polarized public opinion (Wanless and Berk, 2017; Allcott and Gentzkow, 2017; Benkler, Faris, and Roberts, 2018). Benkler, Faris, and Roberts' study during the 2016 US presidential election focused on disseminating information from news media, partisan media, and social networking sites (Facebook and Twitter). They found that propaganda messages disseminated through networks of right-wing media resonated with information from what they called "fake news entrepreneurs," who used clickbait articles to engage readers on social media.

A study on political memes by an extremist group in Britain shows that meme is an effective medium to carry propaganda messages. It can simplify a complicated message in a single picture, carry satire, jokes, or hate speech from the cultural context of its creators, and it can be modified by the readers and create virality (Sparkes-Vian, 2018). In participatory propaganda, the audience can be "swayed and co-opted" into creating digital content and spreading it through their social networks (Wanless and Berk, 2017). At some point, the term "participatory" itself means that audiences deliberate to interpret the propaganda messages and later create content on digital platforms based on their understanding. In other words, the audience is no longer seen as the object of propaganda but can play the part of an active subject (Wanless and Berk, 2017). Audiences can also counter propaganda with content they have created and promote those messages on their social networks. Besides the ability to initiate and engage audience participation, participatory propaganda has a further objective to move its targeted audience to act, not just merely to shape their opinion and beliefs (Asmolov, 2019). The end means of participatory propaganda in the digital era is to divide groups within the community by continuously socializing and internalizing conflict among them (Asmolov, 2019). With many features to create and modify messages—from editing tools, photo manipulation, stickers-making, to deepfake technologies—the audience can participate in producing and distributing fake news and propaganda messages.

Propaganda Strategies in the Digital Era

In the early development of propaganda theory in the United States, debates about its impact on democracy centered around protecting the public from propaganda (Baran and Davis, 2012). Scholars such as Lasswell and

Lippmann argued that democracy would not survive if propaganda continued to use lies and deception to manipulate people. On the other hand, scholars from public education backgrounds, like John Dewey, believed that the public needed to be educated on how to recognize and counter propaganda (Baran and Davis, 2012). In 1937, the Institute of Propaganda Analysis was established in the United States to assist the public in identifying propaganda. The institution identified at least seven common propaganda strategies (Baran and Davis, 2012): name-calling, glittering generalities, transfer, testimonials, plain folks, bandwagon, and card stacking, as explained in chapter 1. These propaganda techniques have persisted and are frequently found in the digital era.

Propaganda strategies in the digital era can be broadly divided into two categories: message strategy, which focuses on the framing and dissemination of information; and virality strategy, which focuses on repetition, amplification, getting the message to be top of mind, and calls to action. The message strategy includes creating fake news, memes, and data leaks (Wenless and Berk, 2017; Sparkes-Vian, 2018; Jalli and Idris, 2019), often using a combination of traditional propaganda techniques. The virality strategy encompasses tactics such as using cyber armies, micro-targeting audiences, bots, trolling, ads, and manipulating platform algorithms (Jalli and Idris, 2019; Wenless and Berk; Neyazi, 2019; Bessi and Ferrara, 2016). In the past, propagandists relied on mass media channels or traditional print media, such as posters and books, to reach audiences. Today, propaganda message distribution is reliant on networks of friends on social media, making the virality strategy crucial to reach both a wider public and specific niche audiences with a strong emotional connection to the message.

Disinformation

As propaganda relies on disinformation to manipulate the public, the digital public sphere suffers from "fake news" aiming to undermine political opponents (Allcott and Gentzkow, 2017). The form of "fake news" or disinformation could vary from a complete fabrication to manipulating some aspects of the information, such as the source, the context, the date, or the quote (Finneman and Thomas, 2018). This disinformation production heavily relies on websites and social media to distribute the messages. In a country where Internet access is poor and the price of having Internet data is high, people rely on social media to get access to news and information. In addition, the hefty monthly payment business model adopted by many online news agencies further barricaded people from accessing quality journalism. When the Rohingya crisis erupted in Myanmar in 2018, many people obtained their news from Facebook without verifying the accuracy of the information, leading to the spread of misinformation in society (in chapter 1, disinformation, misinformation, and mal-information are defined). In 2016, only about 23 percent of people in Myanmar had Internet access, and many of them considered information on Facebook as news (Hogan and Safi, 2018). At that time, propaganda sponsored by Myanmar's armed forces was circulated on Facebook, and the platform failed to detect and address the proliferation of fake news and hate speech, thereby amplifying the propaganda (Milmo, 2021; Guzman, 2022).

In 2017, the Indonesian National Police (POLRI) arrested a group called Saracen, which systematically produced and distributed disinformation on social media. The group coordinated around six Facebook accounts to spread hate toward ethnic and religious groups to its 800,000 followers (BBC Indonesia, 2017). A year later, the POLRI arrested another propaganda organization that utilized networks through the WhatsApp messenger application called the Muslim Cyber Army (MCA). The MCA had been operating since 2014 and aimed to attack ethnic and religious groups as well as the government (Lamb, 2018). According to the POLRI, they work on various issues, but primarily focus on political issues, government policy, and elections. In response to these arrests, in 2019, Meta closed around 2,000 Facebook and Instagram accounts that displayed inauthentic coordinated behavior, including the entire Saracen-linked network (Meta, 2019). Social media platforms remain the primary means of spreading fake news, as people rely on these platforms for information. A survey of well-educated groups in Indonesia found that respondents tended to believe that the information they received from social media was reliable, leading them to continue reading and sharing hoaxes from social media (Khan and Idris, 2019).

Besides spreading hate speech and attacking targeted groups, spreading disinformation during election time can also aim to keep the enthusiasm of the candidate's supporters and mobilize support (Kalsnes, 2016). Distribution and amplification of disinformation on social media during the general elections in Malaysia in 2018 and in Indonesia in 2019 were at least conducted strategically in three ways (Jalli and Idris, 2019). The first strategy was to use fake accounts to create and amplify deceitful messages through the accounts. The second was trolling a prominent politician through Twitter mentions from armies of fake accounts. The third was promoting hashtags to go viral using groups of supporters, either real people, fake accounts, or bots. Social media serves as an intermediary agenda-building platform, which enables disinformation to go viral. High virality plays a crucial role in getting the mass media's attention and promoting certain agendas through false information.

Memes, Stickers, and Emoticons

For many, meme is often understood as funny images or pictures shared on the Internet. However, a meme can actually be any form of content that is widely shared and replicated online, including pictures, links, or videos (Brodie, 2009). This type of medium represents the participatory culture of audiences, characterized by the ability of audiences to interpret, create, and distribute their messages. A meme also triggers and facilitates the *playfulness* concept of new media platforms. These characteristics make memes one of the most popular means to carry propaganda messages, including extremist ideology, political satire, and hate speech (Shifman, 2014; Silvestri, 2015).

Although memes can be easily found on the Internet, their distribution has become even more convenient and faster through messenger platforms such as Line, WhatsApp, and Facebook Messenger. In 2020, sticker sales contributed $200 million to Line's revenue (Deck, 2022). The popularity of stickers is largely due to the large number of messenger users globally, with Indonesia having the third-highest number of WhatsApp users in the world, after India and Brazil (Katadata, 2021). Today, stickers can also be added to Instagram and Facebook stories. They have *playfulness* features that allow users to tell stories and express emotions, and they are also collectible and can be shared. Messenger users can even create their own stickers from any picture by using cutting and editing tools on sticker maker websites and apps.

Like traditional GIFs, memes and stickers also carry symbolic meaning that can be easily used to convey hidden messages, whether to evoke emotions or reduce social tension during interpersonal interactions (Susanto, 2018). In the Philippines, during a political movement to oppose the Anti-Terrorism law, youth protested on TikTok by using emoticons and the word "buzz" in comments (Jalli, Leong, Camba, and Chee, 2021) to avoid negative consequences from the government. By repeatedly commenting using emojis and keywords, TikTok users hoped that their videos would appear in the "For Your Page (FYP)" or timeline without being detected as supporting the protest. While political stickers, which carry political statements or messages, have been around for a while (Wong, 2015), the focus on political memes has mainly been on the GIF format. In countries like Indonesia, where WhatsApp is a major online communication channel, stickers are used and interpreted as a form of political communication (Hidayat, 2022). According to Indonesia's Information and Electronic Transaction Law (UU ITE), a sticker can also be categorized as a medium of communication.

During the presidential campaign in 2019, WhatsApp groups were sites of heated political debates and clashes (Jakarta Post, 2019), causing many people to leave the groups (Tapsell, 2019). Memes, particularly pictures and stickers featuring politicians and public figures, were widely circulated to evoke emotions and fuel hate. Figure 2.1 illustrates WhatsApp stickers of Indonesian politicians that were circulated on WhatsApp groups. The picture on the left is the Governor of DKI Jakarta, Anies Baswedan (2017–2022), edited into the face of Indonesian comedian Gogon, who was known for his crested hair

Figure 2.1 Pictures of Indonesian Politicians Anies Baswedan (Left) and Jokowi (Right) as WhatsApp Stickers. *Source:* WhatsApp 2018.

and Hitler-like mustache. While the picture on the right is President Jokowi with a frowning forehead, accompanied by a text that says: "I don't know, why do you ask me. . . ." The text itself was Jokowi's famous quotation. For example, in 2021, one of the most controversial policies of the Indonesia Corruption Eradication Commission (KPK) was when 56 employees, including investigators and leaders involved anti-corruption, were discharged because they did not pass the post-test nationalism. That time, the public reacted and asked for Jokowi to intervene in the decision, but he vaguely answered by saying his famous quotation: "I don't know, why do you ask me" (Sunaryo, 2019; Nugraheny, 2021). As the debates in a close circle of friends or family are heated on WhatsApp groups, memes could be an effective medium to state support or dissent without having to declare or elaborate further explanations. It is suitable for propaganda because the symbol will surpass rational thinking and argument; otherwise, it will help strengthen the feelings.

Messenger platforms such as WhatsApp are strategic places for propagandists to influence people's opinions and fuel conflicts, as these platforms are mainly used for communication within close social networks such as extended family, work colleagues, religious communities, ethnic communities, school alumni, or interest groups. According to Rogers and Kincaid (1981), close social networks function to provide psychological support and build trust, making some members within the group act as opinion leaders, effectively influencing others. Shaping and winning opinions within WhatsApp groups is crucial during elections, as voters often rely on these networks to decide which candidate to vote for. In countries where WhatsApp is popular, political candidates often establish special teams to disseminate messages and influence opinions through this platform (Evangelista and Bruno, 2019; Maweu, 2019; Tapsell, 2018).

A 2022 study by Baulch, Matamoros-Fernandez, and Suwana found that memes were used as a persuasion tool during the 2019 Indonesian election.

A team of 200 people spread memes on WhatsApp to support Jokowi-Ma'ruf Amin through three layers: creating the narrative, creating the memes, and disseminating them to specific groups. Negative messages and disinformation were also spread about opponents. WhatsApp groups, until now, are still fertile grounds for propagandist messages due to its popularity and ability to target niche audiences, as well as its features such as stickers and the ability to share various types of media including text, doc files, PDFs, images, and videos.

Data Leaks

During the 2016 US presidential election, data leaks were used as a propaganda strategy. One example is the leak of Hillary Clinton's emails, as described in a 2018 study by Benkler, Faris, and Roberts. Wardle and Derakhshan (2017) define data leaks as "mal-information," which is when "genuine information is shared to cause harm, often by moving private information into the public sphere" (pg. 5) (see also the definition of mal-information in chapter 1). This strategy was used as a campaign to damage Clinton's reputation and successfully drew attention from the audience and media. A study by Watts and Rothschild (2017) found that Clinton's email leak received more news coverage than any of Donald Trump's scandals.

The use of data leaks as a propaganda strategy has a long history, dating back to the eighteenth century, when state correspondences in the United States were stolen and published in colonial newspapers (Castronovo, 2014). Today, with digital data storage systems and the proliferation of hackers, data leaks can spread rapidly. In the context of propaganda, the main goal of data leaks is to distract public attention and tarnish the reputation of public figures. Therefore, the focus of news coverage is on the leaked information rather than the leakers. Bjola and Pamment (2018) argue that this focus on the object of the leaks allows authorities to leak information and evade responsibility. This was evident during the Iraq war, when many leaks were broadcast on mass media to support the US government's narrative.

In the digital age, the audience plays a major role in distributing and interpreting leaked information. With smartphones, leaks that tap into latent social issues can turn Internet users from passive audiences into Internet trolls and cause the leaks to go viral. In Indonesia, a predominantly Muslim country, leaks related to religion can provoke the audience to attack the subject of the leaks. One notable example is the case of Ahok, a former Christian governor of DKI Jakarta, who was recorded during a work trip saying that some Muslim preachers used verses from the Quran to deceive voters into not choosing a non-Muslim leader (Sasongko, 2016). The video, which was edited and given the title "blasphemy against religion" by a team member of Ahok's opponent, was then uploaded to social media and went viral (Wijaya, 2016). Two months later, thousands of Muslims, who were primarily recruited through social media, called themselves "the 212 movement" and protested around the national monument, demanding that the government prosecute Ahok. This propaganda against Ahok backfired when a screenshot of a pornographic chat involving the leader of the 212 movement, Rizieq Shihab, and a woman was leaked and circulated on social media. In 2019, another leak involving one of the Muslim leaders in the movement went viral on social media. The video shows Ma'ruf Amin, Jokowi's vicepresidential candidate, telling preachers that Ahok was the main source of conflict in Indonesia and had to be stopped (Rahayu, 2019). Ma'ruf Amin later explained that he was only pointing to Ahok and not Jokowi, even though both were part of the team as Jakarta's governor and vice-governor.

Cyber Armies

Dominating public discussion by deploying cyber armies (or social media troops) is also one of the propaganda strategies. To keep a favorable image, politicians or governments carry and build their narratives on social media. For instance, in Indonesia, the government wanted to project that they work hard for the people. All messages on social media emphasized the government's performance and adopted frames that propagated the same message used by President Jokowi toward its administration: *Work. Work. Work* (Idris, 2019). The Indonesian government also established a social media team in each government agency tasked with disseminating government information and countering criticisms. This team, called Siman ASN ("Sinergi Media Sosial Aparatur Sipil Negara"/collaborated social media team of government agencies), was established by the Ministry of Communication and Information and the Coordinating Ministry of Politics, Law, and National Security. It is active in spreading government information, especially to counter criticisms (Idris, 2019). In some countries, especially with cheaper labor, cyber armies were bots that automatically amplify messages and individuals who were recruited to amplify messages by retweeting them or sharing a post from multiple Facebook pages managed by one account. Neyazi's study (2019) on the India-Pakistan conflict shows the utilization of algorithms and real people in promoting messages on social media.

A study by an Oxford University researcher in 2019 called Global Inventory of Organized Social Media Manipulation, mentioned the use of cyber armies in Indonesia. As the title suggests, the report examines the global phenomenon of being organized into using "troops" on social media to manipulate the conversation. In Indonesia, the use of cyber armies is actually not a new phenomenon. Lim's research (2017) during the 2017 DKI Jakarta

Pilkada mentioned an attempt to manipulate social media content by using a social media buzzer.

But what exactly is meant by buzzer? The term "buzzer" was originally known in marketing because of the need to get the audience's attention regarding promotional messages. With the large production and circulation of information on social media, effort is needed so that a message can reach as many audiences as possible. In his book, *The Marketplace of Attention* (2014), James Webster says that audiences' attention can be obtained from the message and structure. A strong message alone is not enough to grab an audience's attention on social media; it takes a structure in the form of the number of followers who clicked on a message, liked it, and re-shared it. That way, the social media algorithm will read that the message is liked and is important to others. The presence of cyber armies is used to manipulate messages to make it seem as if they are liked by many people and will continue to appear on the timeline. Because the goal is for a message to go viral, buzzers are no longer just humans but can also be bots—computer programs designed to amplify messages. Until now, buzzers have been present and have increased in number because social media platforms allow anonymous or fake accounts.

In the context of Indonesia, cyber armies are now not only buzzers but also opinion leaders on social media (social media influencers). The two-step flow of communication theory says that the effect of mass media on the public is indirect; it affects opinion leaders first before it reaches the targeted audience. Opinion leaders could be anyone who can influence their peers, such as religious leaders, community leaders, public officials, or celebrities. On social media, messages usually come from opinion leaders and get amplified by buzzers to make a message go viral. The buzzer's primary purpose is to build a public agenda that an issue is important and must be discussed by the public. Influencing the public agenda in the media is actually nothing new. The history of media development notes that whenever there is a new medium—for example, newspapers, radio, or television at that time—then every citizen also sees a new public sphere (a new public sphere) where we can discuss more freely. Therefore, mastering each of these new spaces has long been the goal of both the government and businesspeople. Influencing the public agenda is important to gain legitimacy for a policy or program. In addition to the main purpose, the buzzer is also often used to "shut down" criticism. The trick is to "attack" a critique together so that the conversation stops or the critic's reputation in the public eye is damaged. These critics can be ordinary citizens, opinion leaders from the opposition, or the mass media.

The question now is: What causes someone to still believe in the information conveyed by the buzzer? Research by Li and Suh (2015) found that at least three factors influence the credibility of information on social media, namely, interactivity, transparency, and the strength of arguments. Social media buzzers are still somewhat trusted because they are generally willing to interact with their followers, for example, by replying to conversations or giving "likes". In addition, buzzers are also somewhat trusted because they seem transparent in mentioning the source of their information; even sometimes they only mention that the source is "someone from the inner circle" of certain political parties. We often encounter buzzers who even present supporting evidence in the form of photos or videos. Buzzers, especially influencers, can also assemble their messages with logical, convincing arguments and evidence that the mass media do not even publish.

Micro-Targeting Audience

One of the prime features of social media is its ability to target a small audience. On Facebook, for instance, a user can use Facebook Audience Insight to determine the target audience when about to boost a post with advertising. With a cheaper cost compared to advertising in traditional news media, a page administrator can divide the audience by their marital status, year of marriage, number of children, interests, and level of education. This microtargeting audience strategy is harmful because it can trap people inside a filter bubble.

Ads

One of the strategies to create high engagement in a social media post is through advertising. As one of the most popular social media platforms in Southeast Asia, Facebook opens opportunities for the government to pay for advertising so that government messages can reach targeted audiences in a global network. In 2017, hundreds of Russia-based accounts put ads on Facebook condemning Clinton's policy, although they were not directly attacking her (Vaidhyanathan, 2017). According to *The New York Times*, the total ad spending was $100,000 and placed in 470 accounts. Facebook's policy on political advertising itself opens opportunities for propaganda messages because of its lack of transparency and privacy violations (Andreou et al., 2019). Thus, it is hard for its users to recognize who put the ads on Facebook (Binford et al., 2020). For instance, in the Indonesian context, government agencies used Facebook ads to boost their messages on government performance, resulting in the top 10 posts about Covid on Facebook in Indonesia, and all were from government accounts (Idris, 2021). It means not only the Indonesian government could have readers on Facebook but also the government could dominate information on the platform.

Manipulating Platform Algorithm

Social media and most digital platforms use algorithms based on users' behaviors to determine the information on the user's timeline and which information is popular. Besides using cyber armies to boost a post, propagandists also manipulate the search engine algorithm by posting their messages on multiple websites and having fake accounts to spread them on social media (Wanless and Berk, 2017; Benkler, Faris, and Roberts, 2018). In the Philippines, for instance, this strategy was used by bots and fake accounts to promote disinformation in favor of President Duterte's campaign against drugs in 2016 (Ressa, 2016). Publishing stories on multiple websites and hyperlinking them on social media will also help make the information credible and bury opposing information.

Social media bots or computer programs have driven hoaxes and misinformation since 2014. Barbera's research in the United States and European countries—United Kingdom, Spain, Netherlands, Italy, and Germany—on thousands of accounts of politicians, political parties, and journalists covering politics shows that the proportion of followers who are classified as bots is relatively high. At that time, in the 2014 Indonesian election, social media accounts that spread hoaxes were generally operated by networks of humans. In developed countries, such as the United States, United Kingdom, and Germany, the minimum wage is much higher than in developing countries like Indonesia. Consequently, paying people to drive social media conversations costs more. Therefore, bots were cheaper than humans or subcontracted the work outside the country. However, recognizing hoax spreader networks by social media bots is easier than recognizing human-managed social media account networks. Conversation networks are formed due to the similarity of interaction patterns between social media users. An interaction occurs, for example, when someone writes a comment, mentions another account name (mention), or shares a message on social media (retweet or share). Users who have the same interaction pattern will then form a conversation cluster.

In a bot-driven conversational network cluster, one account is centrally positioned, and the other accounts will be connected only to that account but not to each other. The most common form of conversation network is a star-shape or star-shaped network, with one central account whose messages are amplified by accounts in the network cluster (Ratkiewics, Conover, Meiss, Gonçalves, Flammini, and Menczer, 2011). If we imagine a social media conversation as a face-to-face conversation, in this cluster, there will be one person who screams in the middle of the crowd, then the people around him will also shout the same thing. Thus, the screams will resound even louder.

In human-driven conversation networks, the interactions are more diverse because they are not just aiming to forward or echo a message, and the interactions formed are not only related to one issue or topic. As a result, the forms of conversation networks will be more diverse, making it more difficult to assess whether the network is manipulated. Hoax distribution networks that humans drive are less suspicious and have a lower risk of being suspended later by social media platforms.

CHAPTER SUMMARY

Propaganda as a method of persuading and manipulating one's thinking and behavior has been evolving due to the advancement of technology. It is now easier to produce, distribute, and amplify propaganda messages to a micro-targeted audience who can be anywhere as long as they have access to the Internet. The old definition of propaganda that required an organized top-down communication flow is no longer suitable in this digital era. The audience can be involved as an active subject in propagating messages and ideas or even countering the propaganda.

In the digital era, propaganda strategies consist of message strategy and virality strategy. Message strategy focuses on framing and manipulating stories, while virality strategy is any strategy that could increase the audience's exposure to the messages. The first one could include fake news, memes, and data leaks. The second includes cyber armies, micro-targeting audiences, bots, trolling, ads, and manipulating platform algorithms.

Chapter 3

Using Social Media as Propaganda Battlegrounds in Southeast Asia

Propagandists' strategic maneuvering of public opinion on social media remains a dangerous threat to democracy in Southeast Asia. Over the years, the strategic use of cybertroopers in Southeast Asian countries has been prominent (ISEAS, 2021; Cheong, 2020; Jalli and Idris, 2019; Hopkins, 2014), especially during election periods. With Internet penetration increasing over the years and the constant growth of social media users, information warfare launched by political actors to demonize their nemeses could be seen across different platforms. Ample evidence exists to show how political entities strategically use social media like Facebook (Shane, 2017), Twitter (Jalli and Idris, 2019), and YouTube (Golovchenko et al., 2020) to push for a political narrative to garner more supporters in the region. The latest tool available for disposal, TikTok (Quintal, 2022; Becker, 2021), provides unique features enabling propaganda to reach a greater audience. In this chapter, we will delve into the strategic use of social media platforms, such as Facebook, Instagram, Twitter, YouTube, and TikTok, by propagandists to disseminate propaganda and influence public opinion in Southeast Asia. Although extensive research has been conducted on the utilization of Facebook, Instagram, Twitter, and YouTube for propaganda purposes, we will provide a concise overview of their role in the Southeast Asian context. Furthermore, we will place a particular emphasis on TikTok, as this emerging platform has received limited scholarly attention with respect to its potential as a hotbed for propaganda in the region.

FACEBOOK, INSTAGRAM, TWITTER, AND YOUTUBE IN SOUTHEAST ASIA

Social media platforms like Facebook, Twitter, Instagram, and YouTube have over the years proven to be effective in assisting propagandists in spreading agendas in Southeast Asia. From helping politicians in the region gain political milestones to win elections, these four platforms are also used by militants and extremist groups to spread their ideologies and recruit loyalists.

To Assist with Electoral Campaigns

Social media platforms like Facebook, Instagram, and YouTube have become tools for political actors and propagandists to influence voters in Southeast Asia. As Internet penetration in the region grows, cyber armies' use for political purposes is becoming increasingly common. Studies indicate that while active social media campaigns may not guarantee electoral success, they can impact public opinion during electoral campaigns (Leng Ho, 2012; Miller and Ko, 2015; Jalli, 2017). In Malaysia, for instance, Facebook significantly influenced the political landscape, with Barisan Nasional losing its two-thirds majority in parliament in 2008 due to opposing political narratives dominating the platform. Following this, former Prime Minister Abdullah Ahmad Badawi acknowledged underestimating social media's power in shaping political discourse, which contributed to Barisan Nasional's loss of its majority for the first time in 51 years (Jalli, 2017). Since then, scholars have observed Barisan Nasional increasing its social media campaign efforts, including forming "cybertroopers" or cyber armies, consisting of fake accounts, anonymous individuals, and social media influencers that spread pro-government propaganda across various social media channels (Mohd Sani and Zengeni, 2010; Gomez, 2014; Hopkins, 2014; Jalli and Idris, 2019; Cheong, 2020).

Similar patterns of political influence through social media are evident in other countries. In the Philippines, the 2016 election of President Rodrigo Duterte was facilitated by the strategic use of Facebook to disseminate populist propaganda, resulting in a landslide victory (Curato, 2017). Duterte's administration heavily relied on cyber armies to counter critical media coverage, silence critics, and spread disinformation by giving them significant control over shaping public opinion on controversial policies and maintaining power. Facebook has played a pivotal role in transforming the political landscape in Southeast Asia, providing users with a platform to share information and allowing the spread of information pollution (Tsalikis, 2019), contributing to democratic decline in weak democracies like the Philippines.

In Indonesia, political actors actively use platforms such as Facebook, Instagram, and Twitter to propagate political narratives. The use of bots and human "buzzers" on these platforms during elections has raised concerns among Indonesian politics observers. Low media and information literacy in the country exacerbates misinformation issues, with social media serving as a fertile ground for propaganda dissemination. During the 2019 presidential election, the Indonesian cyberspace was inundated with misinformation, including hoaxes and political propaganda supporting presidential candidates Joko Widodo (Jokowi) and Prabowo Subianto (Safitri et al., 2021). Scholars have extensively studied the information warfare between political factions during the 2019 Indonesian presidential election (Jalli and Idris, 2019; Irawanto, 2019; Safitri et al., 2021), discovering that disinformation was strategically employed to demonize candidates. For instance, in the 2019 election period, long-term disinformation about Jokowi being a secret Christian Chinese and a communist sympathizer was resurrected and disseminated by Prabowo's cyber armies (Safitri et al., 2021). Jokowi's camp also spread hoaxes smearing Prabowo, accusing him of enlisting Russian propaganda to aid his campaign (Sapiie and Anya, 2019) and labeling him pro-LGBTQA+ and an infidel after a photo of Prabowo wearing a cassock (priest's robe) went viral in December 2018, distancing him from his strong support base among Islamic fundamentalists (Safitri et al., 2021).

The term "hoaxes" is commonly used in Indonesia to describe information pollution, which includes misinformation, disinformation, and mal-information. Over the past decade, as social media has grown in popularity in Indonesia, the use of hoaxes as a propaganda tool has become increasingly prevalent in the country's politics. Recognizing that information warfare on social media could influence election outcomes, both presidential candidates formed unofficial teams to monitor all social media platforms, analyze public sentiment, and develop strategic action plans. Jokowi's underground monitoring team, "Awan" (cloud), was responsible for analyzing public sentiment on social media, monitoring hoaxes aimed at Jokowi, and relaying data from social media analysis to ground teams, such as "Cakra," for execution (Irabowo, 2019).

The intensity of information warfare during the 2019 presidential election led to significant unrest, with Prabowo loyalists taking to the streets in Jakarta and other provinces, alleging foul play when the polling results were announced on May 21, 2019. According to the official electoral results, Jokowi won over 85 million votes, more than half of the 154 million votes cast during the election. However, Prabowo refused to accept the results, citing widespread cheating and irregularities (Jefriando and Asmarini, 2019). During the protests, demonstrators chanted slogans of economic nationalism and anti-China sentiment, criticizing Jokowi's deals with Chinese firms and insinuating that China had influenced his campaign. This highlights the effectiveness of Probowo's loyalists' disinformation campaign on social media, which portrayed Jokowi as a communist sympathizer (Barahamin and Chew, 2019). The riots resulted in six protesters losing their lives and hundreds sustaining serious injuries (Soeriaatmadja and Chan, 2019).

These events demonstrate that online disputes, uncontrollable propaganda, hoaxes, and information manipulation can spill over into the offline world, jeopardizing national security and public safety, particularly in weak democracies and authoritarian states. This underscores the need for improved media and information literacy, as well as responsible social media use and regulation, to mitigate the potential consequences of information pollution on political stability and public safety.

However, completely stopping the spread of propaganda on the Internet is nearly impossible, as various factors allow it to continue flourishing. One such factor is the propaganda economy—working as a propagandist or contracted social media army member can be lucrative, particularly in lower-income countries like many in Southeast Asia.

In countries like Indonesia, being a social media buzzer or cyber army member can be a well-paid job. In 2016, an anonymous Instagram account, @ sr23_official, gained notoriety for spreading emotionally charged content and attempting to incite division among Indonesian netizens. With over 69,000 followers, @sr23_official posted pictures and writings containing criminal acts, misinformation aimed at causing hatred or hostility toward individuals and community groups based on ethnicity, religion, race, and between groups, disseminated pornography, and spread hoaxes. This content helped the account grow significantly in a short time (Putra, 2018). Examples of contentious captions used by the account included "Chinese are communists," "Government officials are infidels," and "Jokowi is a communist" (Santoso, 2018). The account also targeted several prominent Indonesian politicians, including President Jokowi (Siahaan and Tampubolon, 2019). The person behind the account created multiple similar Instagram and Twitter accounts, collectively garnering over 100,000 followers (Putra, 2018; Santoso, 2018).

The Indonesian police alleged that the creator of the sr23 accounts aimed to establish a powerful online presence with a large following in order to be recruited by the government's adversaries as a professional buzzer (cyber army). Buzzers, who remain anonymous while amassing followers on multiple accounts, can capitalize on the income that spreading content and associating with influential accounts generates. Professional buzzers, hired to create smear campaigns or "hoaxes"" on social media, have become a fixture in Indonesia's political scene. Buzzing rates can range from $300 to $1,500 per month (Jalli and Idris, 2019).

Although buzzing is not illegal in Indonesia, spreading false or defamatory information is. On October 15, 2018, the operator of the sr23 accounts on Instagram and Twitter was arrested by Indonesian authorities for inciting hate and disseminating false information that threatened national security. The individual was charged under the Indonesian Electronic Information and Transaction Law, as well as the Law of the Republic of Indonesia and the Indonesian Criminal Code, for content related to race, religion, and pornography.

To Radicalize

Radical groups, including militants and terrorist organizations, are known to harness social media platforms like Facebook, Twitter, Instagram, and YouTube to spread their ideologies throughout Southeast Asia. Research shows that groups such as DAESH (also known as ISIS) and Al-Qaeda have leveraged social media for the radicalization and recruitment of followers and sympathizers, as well as for fundraising in countries like Malaysia, Singapore, Indonesia, the Southern Philippines, and Southern Thailand.

DAESH, for example, has become infamous for its strategic use of social media by disseminating propaganda, showcasing brutal acts, and promoting its extremist ideology. Scholars have noted that these groups utilize an effective recruitment model to indoctrinate and attract followers in Muslim-majority regions across Southeast Asia by exploiting social media. By fostering a sense of identity, belonging, and purpose for their target audience, extremist organizations can more readily radicalize individuals and extend their reach.

Similarly, Al-Qaeda emerged as a radical group from the anti-Soviet jihad in Afghanistan during the 1980s (Byman, 2015). Like DAESH, Al-Qaeda has employed social media to disseminate its propaganda in countries such as Malaysia, Singapore, Indonesia, the Southern Philippines, and the Southern Thai region of Patani. This approach has enabled them to radicalize people, recruit new followers and sympathizers, and raise funds (Samuel, 2016; Singh, 2016; Hu, 2016; Moir, 2017; El-Muhammady, 2017).

Scholars have observed the successful recruitment model used by Islamic radical groups to indoctrinate and enlist followers in Muslim-majority regions throughout Southeast Asia via social media platforms. This trend of radicalization on social media has alarmed Southeast Asian governments, prompting them to implement stringent monitoring measures to curb the spread of extremist ideologies in the region. The rise of neo-jihadism over the past two decades has been particularly evident in these five countries, with terror cases such as the abduction cases by Ja'maat Abu Sayyaf (officially known as Islamic State (IS)—East Asia Province) in Mindanao, Philippines (McKirdy, 2016), the 2002 Bali bombings by Jemaah Islamiyah (an Indonesian-based terror group associated with Al-Qaeda) (Acharya, 2006), and Southern Thai insurgencies by Patani-separatist groups (Nielson and Hara, 2017). Authorities have foiled some terror plots, such as Singapore's terror plots to attack specific communities' houses of worship in 2020 and 2021 (Singapore Internal Security Department, 2021) and the arrest of

Al-Maunah members in Malaysia after stealing weapons and thousands
of bullets from a Malaysian army camp in Perak in 2000 (Abdul Hamid,
2020). Neo-jihadism is defined as "a religious, political, paramilitary, and
terrorist global movement, a subculture, a counterculture, and an ideology
that seeks to establish states governed by laws according to the dictates
of selectively literal interpretations of the Qur'an and the traditions of the
Prophet Muhammad, through enacting violence" (Peter Lentini, 2008, p.
181). See figure 3.1.

In another example from Indonesia in 2018, authorities uncovered a covert
disinformation operation aimed at destabilizing the Indonesian government
and corrupting the nation's political process. A network of self-proclaimed
cyber-jihadists known as the Muslim Cyber Army (MCA) systematically
spread hateful propaganda on social media platforms such as Facebook, Twitter, and WhatsApp, with the intent to inflame religious and ethnic discord,
provoke paranoia toward the LGBTQA+ community, and defame President
Jokowi by accusing him and the Chinese community of being communists.
This network was orchestrated through a WhatsApp group called "Family
MCA," where inflammatory and divisive messages were shared among group
members. Hateful messages expressing discontent with President Jokowi's
administration and the Chinese communities were inappropriately connected
with persecution crises in countries like Myanmar (Rohingya crisis) and

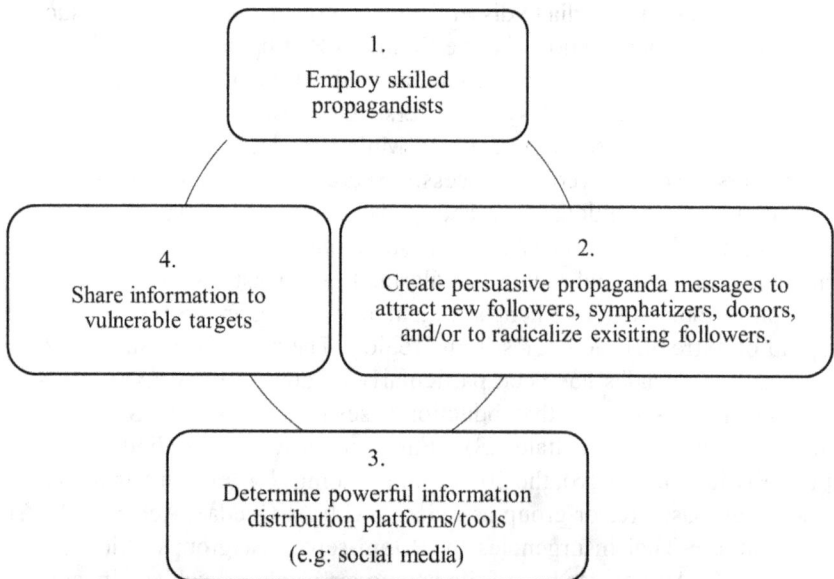

**Figure 3.1   Radical Groups Recruitment and Radicalization Model in Southeast Asia
Loosely Adopted from El-Muhammady (2017).** *Source: Created by the authors.*

Palestine. Local police reported that posts tweeted by MCA on Twitter for around five months were published by bots and semi-automated bots. Posts were often identical, featuring similar texts, memes, or hashtags repeated numerous times (Lamb, 2018).

Radicalization by other religious groups has also occurred in other parts of Southeast Asia, such as in Myanmar, where social media, particularly Facebook, has been used by Buddhist extremists to disseminate hate speech and promote anti-Muslim narratives. This has led to multiple deadly riots in the country over the years. While anti-Muslim conspiracy theories and propaganda began circulating among Myanmar's Buddhist majority in the 1950s, primarily through sermons and speeches by radical monks (Foxeus, 2021), social media has amplified this radical discourse, creating a deeper divide between Buddhists and Muslims (Fink, 2018). Anti-Muslim propaganda pushed by Buddhist ultranationalists, particularly from groups like the 969 movement and Ma Ba Tha, has polluted Facebook with fear-mongering messages and hate speech targeting Muslim communities. They have strategically used Facebook to normalize violence against Muslim minorities (especially the Rohingyas) in the country (Foxeus, 2021).

TIKTOK AS A NEW TOOL FOR PROPAGANDA IN SOUTHEAST ASIA

ByteDance, a Beijing-based tech company, launched TikTok in 2017 as an international version of its popular Chinese app, Douyin. While both apps are technically similar, they run on separate servers, with Douyin adhering to China's media regulations (Niewenhuis, 2019). TikTok has seen a surge in popularity across Southeast Asia, especially during the global COVID-19 outbreak in 2020. Despite initial skepticism about the Chinese-made app, it has been downloaded over 360 million times in the region, with half of the total downloads coming from young Indonesians (Potkins, 2020). TikTok's active users are spread across countries such as Indonesia, Vietnam (Briain, 2021), Thailand, and Malaysia. To encourage more downloads, the app restricts certain features on web interfaces, including the ability to search for specific content on its desktop version (Green, 2020). This limitation has contributed to the app's massive global adoption, making it the sixth most-used social platform (Cyca, 2020).

TikTok as a Space for Propaganda

Unlike its predecessor, TikTok is relatively new in the global-fame game after a sudden burst of new downloads worldwide at the beginning of the

COVID-19 pandemic (Jalli, 2021). While tech companies like Facebook, Twitter, and Google have taken serious steps to combat the misuse of their platforms by propagandists (Bradshaw, Bailey, and Howard, 2021), TikTok, however, was condemned for not having such rigorous policies. In recent years, TikTok has been heavily criticized by scholars and media for allowing extremism on its platform, which led the tech company to rebut with improved policies through their community guidelines (Peter, Fishbein, and Nunu, 2021). Relying primarily on in-house and artificial intelligence (AI) monitoring frameworks and community flagging systems as an audio-visual platform, TikTok seems to struggle to oversee the content its users produce on its platform. With its audience-tailored algorithm, propaganda can result in extremism among fanatical followers. Learning users' preferences for certain content, TikTok's recommendation system would push for similar videos for the users, eventually creating an information bubble that would feed users with certain narratives and influence their hile tech giants like Facebook, Twitter, and Google have taken serious steps to combat the misuse of their platforms by propagandists (Bradshaw, Bailey, and Howard, 2021), TikTok has faced criticism for its less rigorous policies. In recent years, the app has been scrutinized for allowing extremism on its platform, prompting the company to update its community guidelines (Peter, Fishbein, and Nunu, 2021). Although TikTok relies primarily on in-house and artificial intelligence (AI) monitoring frameworks and community flagging systems, the platform has struggled to effectively oversee user-generated content. With its audience-tailored algorithm, propaganda can lead to extremism among fanatical followers. TikTok's recommendation system creates an information bubble that feeds users certain narratives, influencing their worldview.

However, political propaganda persists on the platform, particularly in the "live" section. The "live feature on TikTok has been used by users in several countries, including the US and Russia, to spread political propaganda (Gilbert, 2022). Unlike uploaded audio-visual content, the live feature poses a unique challenge due to its real-time streaming nature, which makes AI monitoring less effective than human content moderation (Dickson, 2019). This issue has been observed on other social media platforms like Facebook (Gomes et al., 2018; Coldewey, 2020), YouTube (Jung and Kim, 2021; Gilbert, 2021), and even TikTok itself (Agate, 2021). Users have exploited these platforms to live-stream graphic content, ranging from mass shootings (Sandle, 2019) to suicides (Dickson, 2020), taking tech companies hours to remove the content.

The Challenge of Content Monitoring on TikTok

For tech companies like TikTok, relying on 24/7 human monitoring of live videos is both unrealistic and economically impractical, given the impossibility of hiring a large enough workforce to monitor the millions of content pieces uploaded daily. A more feasible approach is to harness community engagement by developing a community flagging system that helps identify content that violates platform policies.

A significant challenge for TikTok's content monitoring is the prevalence of indigenous languages, which can easily circumvent the platform's community guideline requirements (Jalli, 2021). There are several ways in which TikTok could be exploited by propagandists to push their agendas, particularly those targeting indigenous communities. AI may struggle to effectively detect audio in these languages, and human fact-checkers may not understand the content unless they are fluent in the specific language or when community members report the content for violating TikTok's policies. This challenge is particularly significant in Southeast Asia, where thousands of native languages are spoken. In Indonesia alone, for example, over 300 languages are spoken by the people across the archipelago (Fettling, 2018). This linguistic diversity provides ample opportunities for political opportunists to use TikTok as a tool for promoting their agendas, making it difficult for the platform to effectively monitor and regulate content.

In 2021, for instance, Myanmar soldiers used TikTok to intimidate citizens amid the military coup in the country (Potkins, 2021). Content uploaded by military officials included blatant propaganda aimed at gaining sympathy from anti-coup protesters, as well as outright threats, intimidation videos, and displays of weaponry meant to forewarn protesters of their willingness to use force (Guest, Fishbein, and Lulu, 2021). In response to these issues, TikTok removed hundreds of such content and began updating its policies, hiring country-specific content moderators and policymakers to better monitor content on its platform.

To tackle these challenges, TikTok and other tech companies could invest in developing more sophisticated AI technology capable of detecting and understanding content in various languages. Additionally, they could strengthen community engagement initiatives by encouraging users to report content that violates platform policies and fostering a collective responsibility to maintain a safe and responsible online environment. This combination of technological advancements and community involvement could help mitigate the risks posed by propaganda and misinformation on social media platforms like TikTok, particularly in linguistically diverse regions like Southeast Asia. By continuously adapting and refining their content monitoring and

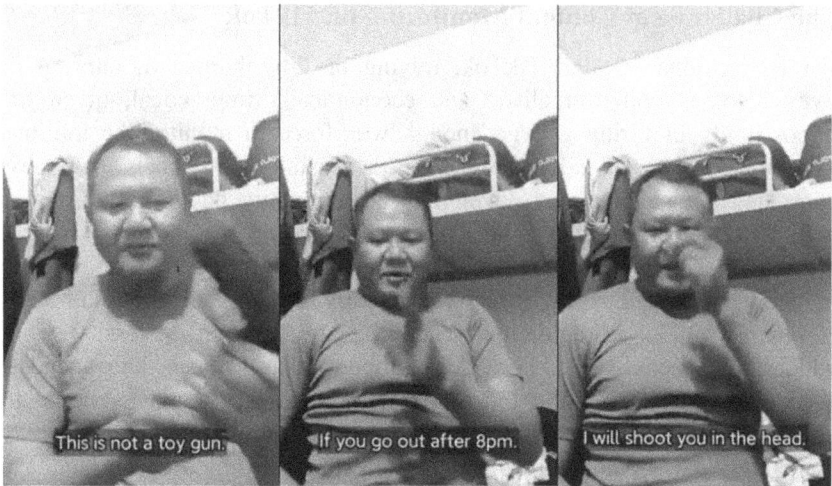

Figure 3.2   In 2021, During the Upheaval Spurred by the Military Coup in Myanmar, Military Officers Were Observed to Use TikTok as a Medium to Launch Threatening Communications Aimed at Anti-coup Protesters. *Source:* Screenshots by authors.

moderation strategies, tech companies can work toward ensuring a safer and more trustworthy digital space for their users. See figure 3.2.

TikTok's Secretive "Heating" Button and Its Implications

TikTok and its parent company, ByteDance, have been engaging in a secretive practice known as "heating," wherein specific videos are hand-picked and their distribution is supercharged to increase their visibility. This is done through manual intervention, ensuring these videos achieve a certain number of views by featuring them prominently on the app's For You page.

Unlike other tech companies that may engage in similar efforts to amplify posts, they usually clearly label promoted content. However, TikTok's heating practices have not been publicly disclosed, raising questions about transparency and fairness within the platform (Baker-White, 2023). While the use of heating has led to potential benefits for some influencers and brands, it has also resulted in employees abusing their privileges and potentially making it difficult for users to distinguish between promoted content and organic content on the For You page. As TikTok continues to gain popularity in Southeast Asia, it is expected that political strategists will use the platform to their advantage, leveraging influencers and cybertroopers in upcoming elections. With the knowledge of TikTok's heating practices, these actors may attempt to manipulate the platform's algorithms and editorial decisions to further their political agendas, reaching a wider audience and potentially swaying public opinion.

TikTok and the Philippines' Presidential Election

As TikTok's popularity continues to rise in the Southeast Asian region, there have been instances where the platform has been used by political propagandists to influence election outcomes. One notable example is the 2022 Philippine election, in which Ferdinand Romualdez (BongBong) Marcos Jr. (henceforth BongBong Marcos) employed TikTok as a strategic tool to reshape the narrative surrounding his controversial family. This ultimately helped him win the Philippine election by a significant margin, garnering 31 million votes, double that of his nearest rival, Leni Robredo (Lema and Dela Cruz, 2022).

Recognizing TikTok's popularity in the Philippines, BongBong Marcos allegedly deployed cyberarmies (propagandists) to create a positive narrative around the Marcos family. This family has been globally known for their involvement in various scandalous cases, including corruption and human rights abuses in the Philippines during the reign of BongBong Marcos' father, Ferdinand Emmanuel Edralin Marcos Sr. Ferdinand Marcos Sr. served as the President of the Philippines from 1965 to 1986 (Celoza, 1997).

By leveraging TikTok's widespread appeal and using cyberarmies to spread propaganda, BongBong Marcos sought to reshape public opinion and distance himself from his family's controversial past. This strategy proved to be effective, as he managed to secure a resounding victory in the 2022 Philippine election. This case serves as a cautionary tale of how social media platforms like TikTok can be manipulated by political actors to further their agendas and influence electoral outcomes, raising concerns about the implications for democratic processes in the region and beyond.

TikTok and Elections in Southeast Asia

As countries like Indonesia and Singapore approach their general elections, the use of TikTok for political lobbying and propaganda is expected to become more evident, based on previous observations of the platform being employed for political purposes (Jalli, 2021). Past research has identified the political use of TikTok in countries like Indonesia, Malaysia, Thailand, and Myanmar, with citizens (including propagandists) disseminating political content on the platform.

For instance, during the Omnibus Law protests in Indonesia, thousands of videos were uploaded to TikTok using popular hashtags such as #tolakomnibuslaw (reject the Omnibus Law), #gagalomnibuslaw (fail the Omnibus Law), and #batalOmnibuslaw (cancel the Omnibus Law). These videos garnered billions of views as President Jokowi's administration announced the ratification of the Job Creation Bill, also known as the Omnibus Law. This legislation, enacted in 2020 as part of economic reforms to attract investors, faced backlash from the public due to human rights and environmental concerns. Over 2 million protesters took to the streets in more than 25 provinces in Indonesia in October, demanding the bill's annulment (CNN Indonesia, 2020).

Demonstrators, advocates, and buzzers actively used TikTok to share content related to the protests, criticize President Jokowi and his administration, and call for street protests across various provinces in Indonesia. Jalli's research (2021) observed that TikTok's recommendation system amplified voices surrounding the Omnibus Law protests, as the algorithm continued promoting similar content (related to the protests) to users who were engaged with it by watching entire videos, liking posts, or leaving comments. The study found that the algorithm not only amplified similar content by pushing these videos to users' "For You" pages (FYP), but it also created an information bubble surrounding the protests. This bubble could lead to civil unrest if propagandists and other users continuously shared emotionally charged content on the platform. As Indonesia, Singapore, and other countries in the region prepare for upcoming elections, the potential for TikTok to be employed as a tool for political propaganda and influence campaigns underscores the need for increased vigilance and regulatory measures to ensure a fair and transparent democratic process. See table 3.1.

During Malaysia's 15th general election, TikTok served as a powerful tool for propagandists, cybertroopers, and loyalists to influence public opinion and sway voters. They exploited the platform to launch smear campaigns against political rivals, spreading misinformation and discrediting opponents through manipulated videos, deepfakes, and doctored images. These tactics effectively sowed doubt and confusion among voters, leading to heated ethnoreligious information warfare on the platform and the emergence of hateful hashtags with ethnoreligious overtones (Jalli, 2023).

The rapid spread of such content highlights TikTok's vulnerability to disinformation dissemination and its potential to undermine the electoral process's integrity. Propagandists and cybertroopers leveraged TikTok's advanced algorithm and highly personalized "For You" page to target specific voter segments with tailored content. By exploiting the platform's data-driven approach, they delivered highly relevant and persuasive messages to individual users, raising concerns about political manipulation and the erosion of informed decision-making among voters.

A study by Jalli (2021) identified several methods used by propagandists to bypass community guidelines on TikTok. They capitalized on trending songs and hashtags to reach larger audiences, employed creative alphanumerical spellings for sensitive words, produced content in indigenous languages, and used the platform's "live"" feature, which presents a unique challenge for AI monitoring systems and human content moderators.

Table 3.1 Top Hashtags Used and Total Views on TikTok Related to the Omnibus Law Protest in Indonesia (2020), Thai Youth Democracy Protest (2020), and Myanmar Military Coup Protests (2021)

Country	Political Events	Top Hashtags on TikTok	Total Views on TikTok
Indonesia	Omnibus Law Protest 2020	#tolakomnibuslaw	2.5 bil
		#Omnibuslaw	1.3 bil
		#tolakombibuslaw	1.3 bil
		#gagalombinuslaw	241.3 mil
		#omnibusciptakerja	206.7 mil
		#batalkanomnibuslaw	116.7 mil
		#menolakomnibuslaw	33.3 mil
		#monibuslaw?	31.3 mil
		#tolakkomnibuslaw	23.1 mil
		#gagalkanomnibuslawciptakerja	18.2 mil
Thailand	Thai Youth Democracy Protests 2020	#เยาวชนปลดแอก (free the youth)	461.3 mil
		#หยุดคุกคามประชาชน (stop harassing people)	181.8 mil
		#ก้าวไกล (move forward)	13.6 mil
		#ไปสภาไล่ขี้ข้าศักดินา (to the council of exile)	9.7 mil
		#ให้จบที่รุ่นเรา (let it end with our generation)	9.6 mil
		#วิโรจน์ (Wiroj)	8.9 mil
		#ปิดสมัยประชุมสภา (Close the session of the council)	2.7 mil
		#รัฐธรรมนูญ (Constitution)	2.6 mil
		#แกรัฐธรรมนูญ (Opposition)	5.4 mil
		#16ตุลาไปราชประสงค์ (16 October to Ratchaprasong)	4.8 mil
Myanmar	Anti-military coup protests	#savemymyanmar	410.9 mil
		#savemyanmar	94.9 mil
		#အမေစုကိုဝန်းရံမယ် (I will protect mother Suu)	5.4 mil
		#whatishappeninginMyanmar	5.3 mil
		#ကမ္ဘာဘာမကမြေဘူး (The world will not end)	4.2 mil
		#စစ်အာဏာရှင်စနစ်ကျဆင်းပါစေ (let military dictatorship fall)	3.2 mil
		#freeaungsansukyi	2.4 mil

Political content on TikTok often escaped the scrutiny of mainstream media outlets and regulatory bodies, enabling propagandists to operate with relative impunity. This lack of oversight raises important questions about the need for greater transparency and accountability in the digital sphere, especially during election periods.

Similar to its predecessors, such as Facebook, Twitter, Instagram, and YouTube, TikTok is increasingly used for propagating political agendas, particularly to attract young voters. The impact of TikTok on the Philippine election in 2022 demonstrates this trend. With the use of deepfakes, paid TikTok influencers, and the potential creation of hype houses to promote political candidates, political parties could orchestrate effective propaganda campaigns to achieve political milestones during election periods.

CHAPTER SUMMARY

Throughout this chapter, it has become evident that propagandists extensively utilize social media to disseminate their ideas and influence public opinion. As communication technology advances, especially with the emergence of user-friendly apps and platforms, information pollution is likely to worsen. The rise of more sophisticated technologies may render automated bots obsolete, resulting in increasingly intricate strategies in information warfare.

As we progress further into the digital age, social media and other Internet platforms will play an increasingly significant role in shaping societal landscapes, impacting everything from politics to the economy. These platforms will become key battlefields for cyber armies and propagandists seeking to advance their agendas and sway public sentiment.

The ease with which misinformation and propaganda can spread across these platforms presents a formidable challenge for regulators, platform owners, and users alike. As technology continues to evolve, so too will the tactics employed by those seeking to manipulate public opinion. This necessitates a proactive and adaptive approach to counter such strategies, including investing in education, digital literacy, and the development of robust fact-checking mechanisms.

Additionally, the responsibility to mitigate the effects of information pollution should not rest solely on the shoulders of platform owners and regulators. Users must also play a role in discerning the veracity of the content they consume and share. Encouraging critical thinking and fostering a culture of skepticism will be essential for combating the spread of misinformation and ensuring a healthy democratic discourse. In conclusion, as communication technology advances and the tactics of propagandists become more complex, it is crucial for all stakeholders—from regulators and platform owners to individual users—to remain vigilant and proactive in addressing the challenges posed by information pollution. Social media and Internet platforms will continue to shape our society, and only through a collective effort can we safeguard the integrity of our democratic processes and maintain the trust necessary for a functioning society.

Chapter 4

Cyberwarfare and Computational Propaganda in Malaysia

Trends and Patterns

In our contemporary world, where interconnectivity is on the rise, cyberwarfare and computational propaganda have become essential elements of modern conflict and information distribution. This has sparked considerable interest from policymakers, researchers, and the general public in understanding the manifestation of these phenomena in various global regions. This chapter aims to introduce you to the context of cyberwarfare and computational propaganda in Malaysia, a nation undergoing rapid digital adoption and technological advancement. Malaysia has persistently worked toward constructing a robust digital infrastructure and promoting extensive Internet access. As the country embraces the digital era, it also faces the challenge of safeguarding its cyberspace from threats posed by cyberwarfare and computational propaganda. This chapter will investigate the trends and patterns found in Malaysia's cyberspace, emphasizing the unique challenges and vulnerabilities this diverse and dynamic nation encounters.

Access to reliable and impartial information is vital for citizens to make informed decisions and engage in the democratic process. The Internet and online communication have significantly broadened access to information, but have also introduced new challenges and risks to democracy. While social media platforms can foster democratic participation by enabling citizens to exchange information and ideas, organize protests and rallies, and hold public officials accountable, they can also be easily exploited, posing a severe threat to democratic health.

In Southeast Asia, the dissemination of propaganda and disinformation has become an increasingly prevalent strategy employed by domestic and foreign actors to influence public opinion and undermine democratic institutions (Lukito et al., 2022; Tan, 2020). These tactics can lead to severe consequences, including the erosion of trust in democratic institutions, increased polarization and division, and the deterioration of democratic norms, ultimately contributing to the rise of authoritarianism. As a rapidly developing nation with a high Internet penetration rate, Malaysia is not immune to the threats of cyberwarfare and computational propaganda (Jalli and Idris, 2019). This chapter will delve into the trends and patterns of cyber operations and computational propaganda in Malaysia, examining the tactics and techniques used by malicious actors and their impact on public opinion.

MALAYSIA AND MEDIA INFORMATION WARFARE

The remarkable growth in Internet penetration and widespread connectivity in Malaysia, with over 90 percent of the population having access to the Internet in 2023, has brought about numerous benefits for the nation. However, it has also inadvertently contributed to the rise of digital propaganda within the country.

As more Malaysians gain access to the Internet and smartphones, they are exposed to an increasing amount of digital content on various platforms, including social media sites and messaging applications. While this has led to greater information sharing and communication, it has also provided a fertile ground for the proliferation of digital propaganda, disinformation, and misinformation campaigns. Malicious actors, both domestic and foreign, have taken advantage of this extensive connectivity to influence public opinion and undermine democratic institutions. They have capitalized on the low media and information literacy levels among certain segments of the Malaysian population, using computational propaganda tactics such as the deployment of bots, the dissemination of false or misleading information, and the manipulation of online narratives. The rapid expansion of Malaysia's digital landscape has made it challenging for the government and relevant authorities to monitor and regulate the flow of information across various platforms. Digital propaganda campaigns can easily cross-platform and gain traction, making it difficult for citizens to discern between authentic and manipulated content.

As Malaysia's digital landscape continues to evolve, propagandists are adopting increasingly sophisticated tactics and strategies. They are leveraging advanced technologies, such as artificial intelligence (AI) and machine learning, to target specific demographics, craft persuasive narratives, and amplify their messages. For instance, the use of deepfakes, the bombardment of false information (the firehose of falsehood as discussed in chapter 1), and the deployment of cybertroopers to shape public opinion are among the numerous techniques employed. In light of the low media and information literacy within Malaysian society, computational propaganda campaigns have become a vital method for propagandists in the country. Computational propaganda, as defined by Howard, Woolley, and Calo (2018), involves the use of computational devices, automation, algorithms, and data analytics to manipulate public life. By exploiting the power of the Internet and social media platforms to disseminate misinformation, amplify specific viewpoints, and influence the behavior of individuals and groups, computational propaganda poses a significant threat to democracy worldwide.

There are various ways to deploy computational propaganda. One common tactic is the use of bots, which are automated accounts that can be programmed to perform a wide range of tasks on social media, such as posting content, commenting, or following other users. Bots can be employed to amplify certain viewpoints or messages by creating the illusion of widespread support for a particular cause or candidate. Another tactic in computational propaganda is the use of disinformation with the goal of creating or amplifying misinformation. This involves generating and distributing false or misleading information with the intent to confuse or manipulate public opinion. Various channels, including social media, websites, and news outlets, can be utilized to achieve this end. According to Bradshaw and Howard (2018), "the term (computational propaganda) encompasses issues to do with so-called 'fake news,' the spread of misinformation on social media platforms, illegal data harvesting and micro-profiling, the exploitation of social media platforms for foreign influence operations, the amplification of hate speech or harmful content through fake accounts or political bots, and clickbait content for optimized social media consumption" (pg. 4).

In Malaysia, computational propaganda campaigns through information manipulation and distortion of truth by cybertroopers actively contribute to the continuous information pollution in Malaysian cyberspace, negatively affecting the health of democracy. While the use of propaganda for political ends is definitely not a recent phenomenon in Malaysia, as over the years, traditional media outlets such as TV, radio, and the printing press have been used as the government's propaganda mouthpieces (Anwar and Jalli, 2020), the availability of social media, high Internet penetration, and increased digital device affordances contribute to the emergence of novel propaganda techniques to influence the Malaysian public. Today, primary information sources for many Malaysians are no longer printed and broadcast on media, which in Malaysia is monopolized by the government, but social media and Internet sites; this makes Malaysians more vulnerable to computational propaganda from various actors. Low media and information literacy in many segments of Malaysian society and vast exposure to Internet content provide a prime opportunity for cyberarmies and political propagandists to stir public opinion to their advantage, particularly during unstable political climates and election periods, undermining the principle of democracy that is supposed to be upheld by a proclaimed democracy like Malaysia.

In Malaysia, social media like Facebook, WhatsApp, Twitter, Telegram, and TikTok are hotbeds for political propaganda. Multiple reports (see Hopkins, 2014; Seiff, 2018; Mustapa Kamal, 2018; Jalli and Idris, 2019; Leong, 2021) have been written on how propagandists, mainly funded by local political actors, focus on creating emotionally charged content rooted in contentious racial and religion-related debates that quickly get the people to rile up against one another, sowing social discord, reflecting the dominant identity politics in the Malaysian political scene.

Another unique feature to consider for a diverse country like Malaysia is the myriad of languages spoken by the people. Particularly in two Malaysian states, Sarawak and Sabah, where dozens of indigenous groups live, propagandists and politicians have to be more strategic in curating their messages, especially knowing the fact that these states have significant influence over general elections, and are historically the two main states that contributed to Barisan Nasional's electoral victories. This affects not only how propagandists should develop their campaigns but also influences the ability of relevant authorities to identify propaganda messages, especially on social media. Consequently, computational propaganda campaigns launched in local indigenous languages and dialects targeting indigenous populations are hard to trace, especially with the built-in analytic tools offered by tech companies (this will be discussed further in this chapter). False narratives and distorted truths propagated by propagandists would remain on social media unless other users reported the content to local authorities or the platform moderators. Worse, with the popularity of encrypted free-text messaging apps like WhatsApp in Malaysia, tracing propaganda campaigns is almost impossible, enabling propaganda-driven misinformation or disinformation to continue influencing public opinion.

The fluidity of Internet content also allows for propaganda to cross-platform, enabling content to gain further traction in the public and damaging the people's ability to make informed decisions, including choosing leaders based on factual information and authentic political debates. Computational propaganda remains prevalent in Malaysia despite current attempts to mitigate information pollution in the country through enacting bills, policies, and concerted efforts by non-government actors. Coordinated computational propaganda campaigns are continuously being used to gain and maintain unchecked power, affirming authoritarianism and contributing to the declining democracy in the country.

Cybertroopers in Malaysia

In Malaysian political warfare, cybertroopers are important to propagate political narratives, influencing public opinion, especially nearing elections.

The combination of cybertroopers, anonymous individuals, and misguided supporters helped elevate politicians, vilify opponents, and eventually impact electoral results. Social media like Facebook, Twitter, YouTube, WhatsApp, and now TikTok are strategically used to share propaganda messages to gain more followers, stifle criticism, and demonize political opponents. Particularly in the case of paid cybertroopers, although denied by political parties that they used cybertroopers to assist with online campaigns, several studies have found otherwise (Hopkins, 2014; Jalli and Idris, 2019). Often fueled by hate speech toward political opponents and driven by misinformation, orchestrated online operations by cybertroopers yield results in Malaysian politics. This was made easier with low media and information literacy in the country, which catapulted the success of such campaigns to a greater level. Computational propaganda through the deployment of cybertroopers, bots, and paid influencers might be subtler, in contrast to a coup, for example. Still, such methods' impact on political ends is equally detrimental to democracy.

"Cybertrooper" is a term used to describe political cyberarmies in Malaysia, firstly associated with Barisan Nasional. Barisan Nasional is a political coalition led by the United Malay National Organization (UMNO) and has been the most dominant coalition in Malaysian history. Since the independence of Malaya (peninsular Malaysia), Barisan Nasional (and its successor, Perikatan Nasional [PN]) has been in power until today, except from 2018 to 2019, when the coalition lost its first general election to the opposition, Pakatan Harapan (PH), which the famous Dr. Mahathir Mohammad led, a former UMNO leader-turned opponent. Unlike avid supporters of political parties, cybertroopers are often paid to spread specific propaganda on the Internet, particularly on social media. While early reports of cybertroopers in Malaysian politics first emerged in 2004 (Cheong, 2021), the use of cybertroopers to help build narratives for Barisan Nasional became evident during the 2008 general election, when the coalition, for the first time in history, lost its two-thirds majority in the parliament (Jalli, 2017). Historically, since independence in 1957, Barisan Nasional had always dominated the two-thirds majority in the parliament; however, due to active online campaigns on social media by opposition parties to rally young and new supporters, the Barisan coalition lost its grip in the parliament (Thien, 2011). After the election, the then leader of Barisan Nasional, Prime Minister Ahmad Badawi, made a stern statement that Barisan Nasional had underestimated the impact of the Internet on Malaysian politics (Hopkins, 2014) and therefore should move forward with strategic plans to harness the power of the Internet, mainly social media like Facebook and Twitter.

There's no secret room somewhere where you open it, and then there are like a thousand people at desktops or laptops, working hard at manufacturing comments and things like that—but definitely we have offices in the party as well as in government departments who are what used to be traditional corporate communications, but now are social media managers who put out the right facts, who try to address misplaced criticisms.—Khairy Jamaluddin, of Barisan Nasional during an interview with Channel News Asia (CNA).

Malaysia's 14th General Election (GE14) 2018

Najib Razak Propaganda and the #1MDB Scandal

During the lead-up to the 14th Malaysia general election in May 2018, the digital war of perception over the One Malaysia Development Berhad (1MDB) scandal involving Prime Minister Najib Razak was rampant on social media. Globally known as one of the key figures in a massive corruption scandal involving the misappropriation of billions of dollars from the fund, including the scandalous "political donation" of $700 million transferred to his personal bank account, Najib Razak had to establish a robust online persona and propaganda campaigns to maintain his power and counter the criticism leveled against him by the public both domestically and internationally since 2016 (Lee, 2016).

Despite the scandal, orchestrated computational propaganda campaigns launched on social media, such as the #respectmyPM campaign and #maluapabossku, helped Najib Razak maintain a positive image among his loyal supporters. According to our earlier research, Najib Razak's troopers claimed they were paid handsomely to create a favorable perception of him while simultaneously character-assassinating his political opponents (Jalli and Idris, 2019).

The cybertroopers we interviewed in the research also shared that several departments were created for this goal, with the central department located in Selangor, Malaysia. Coordinated meetings of cybertroopers, either face-to-face or via WhatsApp groups, helped create consistent narratives about Najib Razak across social media ahead of the general election. Besides Facebook, Twitter, Instagram, and YouTube, WhatsApp was one of the key platforms for Najib Razak's cybertroopers to spread pro-Najib Razak propaganda (Tiung, Idris, and Idris, 2018). WhatsApp is the number one free messaging app in Malaysia; therefore, sharing propaganda on WhatsApp would be a smart move for Najib Razak's cybertroopers. In addition, with WhatsApp's end-to-end encryption feature, messages transmitted on the platform are protected from public search, making propaganda messages harder to detect by fact-checkers and scholars (Bradshaw and Howard, 2018).

During our conversation with a former Barisan Nasional cybertrooper, they revealed that they collaborated in groups to micro-profile individuals on WhatsApp and share pro-Barisan propaganda. In these groups, they would "broadcast" messages to multiple users and hope that they would forward the pro-Barisan propaganda, primarily related to Najib Razak's 1MDB scandal, to other WhatsApp groups they belonged to. The cybertroopers would repeat this daily with some targeted individuals, including journalists and media professionals. Our informant stated that several WhatsApp groups were created to include targeted journalists from various media houses around the country, and they would be provided with doctored pictures, edited videos, and false allegations about opposition leaders.

The goal of this tactic was to get journalists and media to write negative reports on opposition leaders. However, according to our informant, it often backfired, as journalists usually questioned the authenticity of the messages they received on random WhatsApp groups they were added to. Like on other social media platforms, Barisan Nasional's WhatsApp propaganda operations are often centered on divisive narratives related to race, religion, and monarchy, resulting in heightened ethnic tensions and revived nationalistic movements in some parts of Malaysia. Smear campaigns on social media near the election are common in Malaysia (Prakash, 2021). These campaigns will continue unless tech companies properly address the existence of propaganda, especially on encrypted platforms like WhatsApp.

2018 #Pulangmengundi Hijack

A few instances of online users silenced by cybertroopers using bots and semi-bot attacks could be seen during Malaysia's 14th general election in 2018. A Twitter influencer, @klubkiddkl or Joe Lee (Joe Lee changed his tweet handle in 2020 to @iamjoelee), the initiator of the trending #pulangmengundi (go home to vote) hashtag in 2018, said that the hashtag was hijacked by cybertroopers after it went trending on Twitter. The hashtag was meant to connect people who needed help to go to their hometowns to vote with people who were willing to help them, either through monetary donations or carpooling together, which was seen as a criticism of the government at that time (Leong, 2019). The #pulangmengundi hashtag came about as a response to the government's announcement (under Prime Minister Najib Razak) to hold the election on Wednesday, May 9, 2018, which was odd for Malaysia as, traditionally, polling is held on weekends, to ease voters' travels to their hometowns where they registered to vote (Seiff, 2018). Critics saw the odd date as a methodological approach by the incumbent Barisan Nasional government to lower voters' turnout, which would help Prime Minister Najib Razak maintain his position, albeit muddled with the global corruption scandal 1MDB at that time. According to @klubkiddkl, as the hashtag gained traction, he noticed that many pro-Barisan Nasional or pro-government tweets used the same hashtag to drown out the call for help to vote and criticism of the government. These anonymous accounts also added hashtags like #SayNotoPH (say no to Pakatan Harapan, which was the leading opposition during the 14th general election) and #RespectMyPM (respect my prime minister) alongside #pulangmengundi on pro-Barisan Nasional tweets.

Hundreds of Twitter accounts shared thousands of such tweets, which were automatically shared with all #pulangmengundi's hashtag followers, drowning out legitimate calls for help and swaying voters to support the incumbent party. As a former paid influencer for several political parties in Malaysia, @klubkiddkl asserted that the modus operandi of using bots and semi-bots to drown out criticisms, particularly on Twitter, is standard for political information warfare in Malaysia (Get Real, 2020). Twitter bots are sophisticated programs that can automatically tweet, reshare, and like posts. They can be programmed to generate up to 2,400 tweets a day and can send these tweets to any number of people who follow the hashtags included in the posts. During the #pulangmengundi cyberattack in 2018, bots were deployed to create noise, push pro-Barisan Nasional propaganda, and stifle the #pulangmengundi movement. Acquiring Twitter bots for propaganda campaigns is relatively easy, as bot programs can be bought in online marketplaces or built by skilled coders. By leveraging the Twitter algorithm, which enables tweets to be quickly shared with a large number of users, deploying bots for propaganda campaigns can significantly influence trend ranking and Twitter schematic. The more content, in this case, hashtags, is shared, the higher it climbs on Twitter's list of trending topics. See figure 4.1.

In response to the attack, @klubkiddkl and other Twitter users collaborated to identify and report suspicious profiles to Twitter using a manual "bot spotting" method. Bot spotting involves scrutinizing social media traffic to identify any unusual patterns. Although detecting basic bot programs on Twitter is relatively simple, more advanced bots often use generic avatars, repeat content, and avoid personalized responses when engaged by other users. As bots become increasingly sophisticated, identifying them is becoming more challenging, even for experts who specialize in bot spotting (Hassan, 2020). In Malaysia, political actors have deployed highly automated bots that mimic human behavior online, further complicating the bot-spotting process (Prakash, 2021).

During the #pulangmengundi campaign in 2018, Twitter depended on its users to flag and report accounts that appeared to be bots or operated like bots to combat information pollution on its platform. Numerous accounts with suspicious names and generic avatars were identified and reported by Twitter users supporting the #pulangmengundi movement. As a result of these reports, Twitter suspended many of these flagged "bot-like" accounts for violating its policies. According to @klubkiddkl, more than 7,000 accounts were collectively reported to Twitter during the #pulangmengundi hijack, and

Figure 4.1   Screenshot of a Tweet Posted by a Suspected Bot on April 15, 2018, Less than a Month Before Malaysia's 14th General Election 2018. *Source:* Jalli (2022).

a significant number of these accounts were subsequently suspended (Get Real, 2020).

Presently, Barisan Nasional is quite transparent regarding the existence of specific departments dedicated to digital operations that serve as the coalition's digital arms. Although Barisan Nasional denied using cybertroopers and bots to influence public opinion during GE14, the coalition has openly sought pro-Barisan Nasional supporters' assistance in online campaigns. These "loyal supporters" are recruited to spread pro-government propaganda and promote artificial narratives, often under the guise of being part of the coalition's online supporters (Get Real, 2020). Opposition parties also use similar tactics through their computational propaganda machinery. See figure 4.2.

For example, former Barisan Nasional cybertrooper, Syarul Ema, also known as Ratu Naga, admitted to managing a network of 80 pro-Barisan Nasional cybertroopers before GE14. Growing up in a family of Barisan Nasional loyalists, Ratu Naga allegedly became a supporter herself, promoting Barisan Nasional policies. According to her, cybertroopers under her command owned multiple social media accounts to spread pro-Barisan Nasional propaganda on Facebook and Twitter. On Facebook, cybertroopers would infiltrate and create groups to promote anti-opposition narratives, uplift Barisan Nasional political candidates, post content supporting Barisan

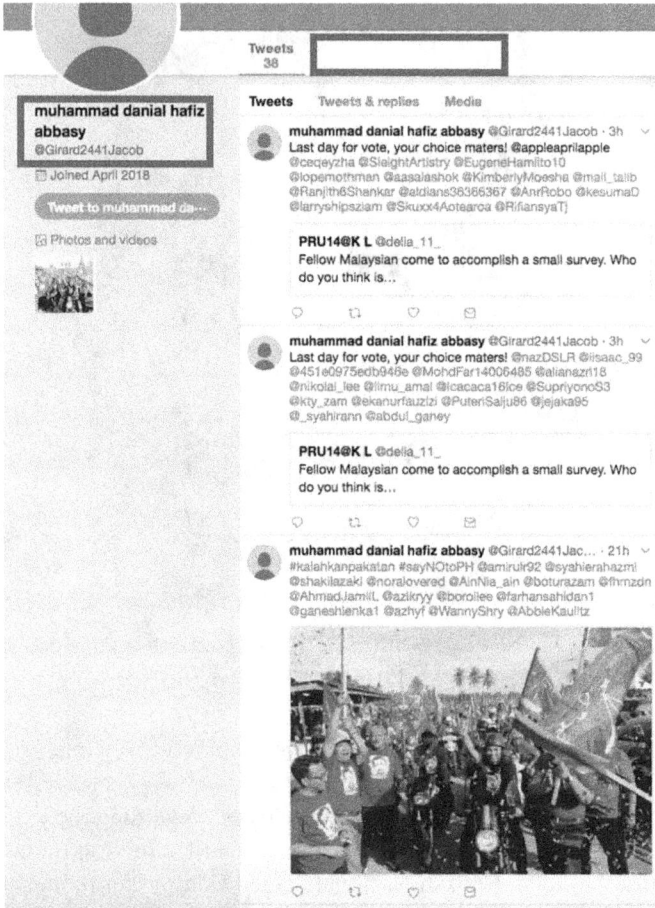

Figure 4.2 Example of Automated Bots Deployed during Malaysian 14th General Election. Signs of Bots for This Account Include No Avatar, an Odd Tweethandle That Doesn't Match the Screen Name @girard2441jacob, Multiple Hashtags, Repetitive Message, and Tagging Several Twitter Users in One Tweet. *Source:* DRFLab (2018).

Nasional propaganda, and collaborate to silence critics. The operation aimed to create negative perceptions of the opposition while cultivating a highly positive image of Barisan Nasional (Get Real, 2020).

> Kita kena create persepsi, supaya orang benci dengan Pakatan Rakyat (we have to create (negative) perception (of Pakatan Rakyat), so the public will hate Pakatan Rakyat. —Ema Syarul former Barisan Nasional's cybertrooper.

To generate engagement and public interest, cybertroopers in Malaysia would analyze current issues of interest and inject provocative content related to sensitive topics such as race, religion, and monarchy to provoke online users into responding (Mustapa Kamal, 2018). As identity politics is a potent force in Malaysia, playing on these sensitive topics would attract more engagement and shape public perceptions of political coalitions and opposition parties. According to Syarul Ema, such methods have helped Barisan Nasional achieve significant political victories since 2011. However, in the 2018 election, Syarul Ema switched her support to PH and collaborated with other cybertroopers and supporters to spread a counter-narrative that encouraged voters to turn out on election day, leading to a massive voter turnout and PH's victory with 82.3 percent of the vote, the third-largest voter turnout since independence (Rahman, 2018). During the election period, political observers and scholars noted intense information warfare between Barisan Nasional's cybertroopers and the opposition's cyber armies. Ultimately, the side with a stronger voice in the digital space and more power over the media would have a tremendous advantage in influencing public opinion (Weaver, McCombs, and Shaw, 2004).

MALAYSIA'S 15TH GENERAL ELECTION (GE15) 2022

During the Malaysian 15th General Election, similar patterns were observed, although the new and intense political warfare took place predominantly on TikTok. As TikTok's popularity increased during COVID-19 lockdowns, cybertroopers and politicians actively used the platform to influence public opinion, sway voters, and spread propaganda during the election. In this recent election, TikTok emerged as a fertile ground for information warfare among competing political parties, and methods such as astroturfing and disinformation were widely used to sway public opinion (Jalli, 2023). Political astroturfing, which involves coordinating a disinformation campaign with participants posing as ordinary citizens acting independently, can have a significant impact on electoral outcomes and other forms of political behavior (Keller et al., 2019). Astroturfing was utilized in Malaysia to create fake grassroots support for certain political parties, particularly due to the emotionally charged content created by cybertroopers, which aimed to misinform and elicit strong reactions from online users. During the GE15 election period, political astroturfing was prominently observed on TikTok, involving loyalists and cybertroopers from the two main contesting coalitions, PN and PH. During the GE15 election period, our investigation of political propaganda on TikTok revealed several propaganda tactics, including astroturfing, name-calling, whataboutism, and disinformation. Malaysia has a history of grappling with inter-ethnic and inter-religious relations, which is viewed as one of the consequences of British colonization and their "divide and conquer" approach (Jalli et al., 2022). The ethnoreligious tensions were particularly conspicuous during GE15, owing to the heightened tension and anticipation surrounding the final election verdict in Malaysia. See figure 4.3A,B.

#13mei1969 Trending on TikTok During GE15

Following the polling day in Malaysia, the Malaysian TikToksphere was inundated with content regarding the "May 13" incident, an unfortunate

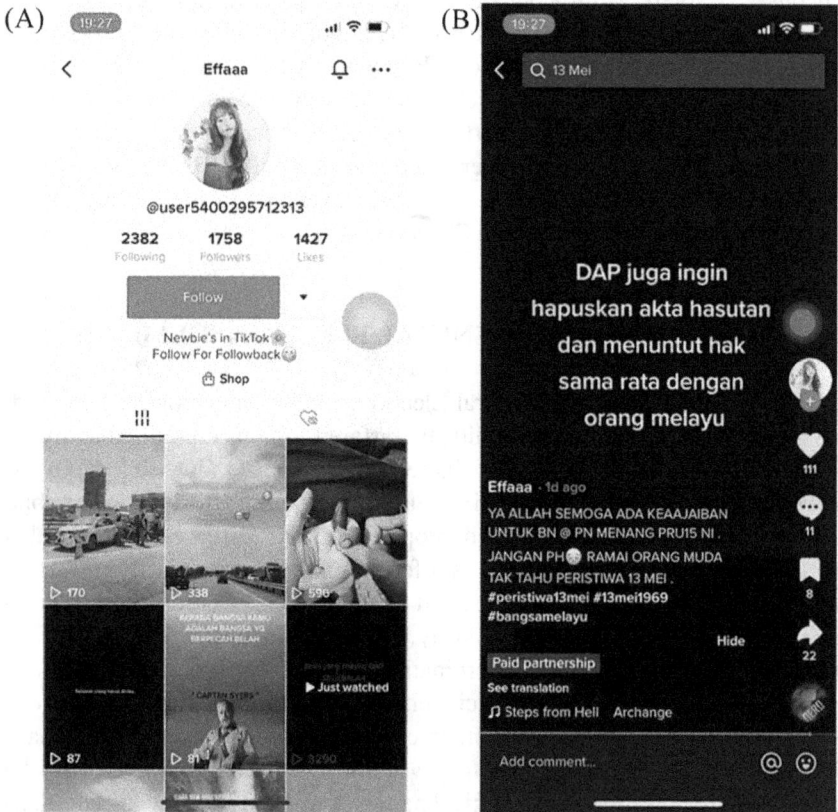

Figure 4.3A,B   (A) TikTok User @user54000295712313 Posted Various Emotive Content on Its TikTok Page (Astroturfing). Their Content Focuses Mainly on Disinformation and Propaganda Campaigns against PH, and One of Its Key Political Parties Is DAP, a Chinese Majority Party. (B) Using the Hashtags #peristiwa13mei, #13mei1969, and #bangsaMelayu (Malay Race), the Video Shared Anti-DAP Propaganda with Various Racially Charged Captions: "DAP juga ingin hapuskan akta hasutan dan menuntut hak sama rata dengan orang melayu" (DAP Also Wants to Abolish the Sedition Act and Demand Equal Rights with the Malays). This Video Also Had "paid partnership" Label on Its Caption, Indicating This Video Was Sponsored. TikTok Did Not Provide Comments. On December 15, This Account Was No Longer Available on TikTok. *Source:* Screenshots by authors.

ethnic conflict that took place in Kuala Lumpur in 1969 between the Malay and Chinese communities. The hashtags #13mei and #13Mei1969 pertain to the tragic May 13 incident, which was an ethnic conflict that transpired in Kuala Lumpur in 1969 between the Malay and Chinese communities (Jalli, 2017). The conflict was initiated by a rally that was organized by Malay political groups on May 12, 1969, to protest the outcome of the 1969 Malaysian general election, in which the ruling *Parti Perikatan* (Alliance Party, Malay-majority party) lost several seats to the Chinese-dominated DAP (Soong, 2008). The rally escalated into a violent confrontation between the two communities, resulting in hundreds of casualties and widespread property damage (Jalli, 2017).

The uploading of #13mei videos on TikTok generated extensive public concern among Malaysian netizens, who accused political figures, primarily from the PN, of exploiting the incident to gain voters' sympathy and foment anti-China sentiment (Latiff and Chu, 2022). The viral hashtags related to May 13 garnered considerable public attention in Malaysia, leading the government to be extra cautious, particularly after several warnings of the possibility of a recurrence of the May 13 racial conflict if the Chinese-dominated DAP and PH were to form a government following the election (Mohsen, 2022). After the emergence of extensive #13Mei content on TikTok, Malaysian authorities reached out to ByteDance, the parent company of TikTok, to monitor hate speech and disinformation on the platform (Latiff and Chu, 2022). Nonetheless, there were allegations that TikTok did not respond quickly enough and even allowed ""paid sponsorship" to creators who openly shared contentious ethnoreligious content. As stated by Ibrahim (2022), after the election (specific number of days unspecified), TikTok's automated system blocked up to 1,126 videos that were deemed provocative and extreme. Before the election date, from November 12 to 18, a total of 857 videos were automatically blocked, while on November 19, an additional 130 videos were taken down (Ibrahim, 2022).

Nevertheless, even though TikTok removed many of the videos related to May 13, several provocative ethnoreligious videos, particularly ones produced in local languages, remained on the platform (Jalli, 2023). This raises concerns about the effectiveness of TikTok's enforcement of their "community guidelines" policy on hate speech, misinformation, and harmful conduct (TikTok, 2022), particularly when it involves minority languages (Jalli, 2020). See figure 4.4A,B.

Propaganda in Indigenous Languages on Social Media

The use of minority languages as a means of effectively spreading propaganda can be a potent tool to manipulate a particular group of people. Minority

Figure 4.4A,B **(A) As of February 3, 2023, Despite TikTok's Policies on Disinformation and Misinformation, Contentious Ethnoreligious Content Remains Available on the Platform. A TikTok Video Posted on November 7, 2022, Which Reads "Haram for Malay Muslim to vote PH." (B) A Caption on the Right, Stating, "Vote for BN parliament member, DAP is anti-Islam, DAP is anti-Malay," Demonstrate That Even Two Months after the GE15 Election, Ethnoreligious Disinformation Continues to Be Present on the Platform.** *Source:* Screenshots by authors.

languages typically pertain to the languages spoken by a smaller subset of individuals within a larger population, which may include indigenous languages, among others. In Malaysia, indigenous languages play a crucial role in East Malaysian politics, given that East Malaysia is comprised of diverse indigenous communities with substantial linguistic diversity, unlike West Malaysia. When propaganda is disseminated in an indigenous language, for instance, it can create a sense of exclusivity among speakers of that language, fostering a stronger sense of community and loyalty to a particular cause or ideology. Additionally, propaganda spread in a minority language can remain undetected by those who do not understand the language, thus making it more potent and successful. Communication strategists and politicians have long understood the power of indigenous languages to mobilize the support of local people (Ojabode and Odalapo, 2014).

In Sabah and Sarawak, winning an election necessitates the utilization of indigenous languages to disseminate a pro-party narrative. This is due to the fact that a significant proportion of the population in both states does not speak Bahasa Malaysia or English as their first language. Moreover, there are several segments of society that do not speak Bahasa Malaysia or English fluently, given that these languages are not their mother tongues. This is particularly true for indigenous people living in rural areas of the states.

By employing indigenous languages in social media campaigns to win over the hearts of indigenous people, politicians can create stronger connections with their constituencies, increase their ethos, and ultimately influence the degree of support they receive (Rjéoutski and Speranskaia, 2015). By producing content in local languages and dialects, propagandists can create a more personal and engaging experience for their audience and elicit a greater emotional response. This approach can be particularly effective in minority communities, like in Sarawak, where the use of a shared language can help foster a sense of solidarity and group identity.

Social media platforms like Facebook, Twitter, and TikTok provide propagandists with a range of tools and strategies for reaching their intended audience, including targeted advertising, content optimization, and algorithmic filtering. By utilizing these features, propagandists can tailor their messages to specific demographic groups and increase the likelihood of engagement and conversion. Several cybertroopers interviewed for this book, who primarily created social media content for Sabah and Sarawak, emphasized the importance of producing persuasive content in local languages and dialects, as content in local languages tends to create stronger engagement and receive higher responses. The cybertroopers found social media platforms such as Twitter, Facebook, and TikTok particularly helpful for evaluating content engagement, as these platforms provide analytic tools to analyze content popularity and user engagement. The use of computational approaches for propaganda or intentional messaging has revolutionized the dissemination of ideas and has proven to be an effective means of sharing political ideologies with targeted constituencies.

It is important for us to be aware of the dominant language spoken in the targeted population. I can't create content in Bahasa Semenanjung (Malaysia) when people speak Iban (one of the Dayak languages) in the longhouses in Kapit (Sarawak). There would be a gap, as they don't feel the sense of closeness to the messenger. Plus, knowing which platform they're on is crucial. I tend to

spend more of my time creating content on Facebook, but less on other platforms like Twitter or YouTube. They're (Twitter and YouTube) not as popular.
—Cybertrooper SBN

East Malaysian politicians have recognized that their political success
largely depends on the support of rural communities. As a result, they
actively utilize indigenous languages in their campaigns, advertisements, and
other mobilization activities. The adoption of local languages by politicians
goes beyond mere linguistic proficiency; it is a strategic and intentional act of
utilizing the people's strengths "against" them (Ojabode and Odalapo, 2014).
What it means in the context of propaganda studies is that, while minority
languages such as indigenous languages can create a sense of community
between the people and politicians and, to a certain extent, a sense of
exclusivity, these languages can also be used to further marginalize already
oppressed groups. In some instances, indigenous languages may not have
the same level of legal protection as majority languages, making it easier for
those in power to silence opposing viewpoints.

In Sarawak, Gabungan Parti Sarawak (Sarawak Party Alliance, or GPS)
has successfully used the Iban language, the primary indigenous language
in the state, to connect with the Iban community, the largest ethnic group
in Sarawak (Lim, 2022). As this community remains a crucial voting bloc
for the political party, maintaining GPS's positive image within the Iban
community is of utmost importance. During the Sarawak state election in
December 2021, GPS loyalists and cybertroopers produced content not only
in English and Malay but also in Iban and other Sarawakian dialects, such as
Bahasa Sarawak.

GPS, formerly known as Sarawak Barisan Nasional (SBN), has held power
in Sarawak since 1974 (Onn and Zhang, 2021) and is currently the fourth-
largest bloc in the Dewan Rakyat (House of Representatives). The political
landscape in Sarawak is unique, with a different demography compared to
other states in Malaysia, as the Dayak community represents about 45 percent
of Sarawak's population, with Malays and Melanau comprising around 30
percent and the Chinese at about 24 percent. In addition, only 30 percent of
the population is Muslim, with the majority of the people being Christians
at around 43 percent (Onn and Zhang, 2021). The diverse population of
Sarawak presents a unique challenge for political parties, especially in
crafting messages that resonate with the majority of the people. Utilizing
indigenous languages and local dialects to propagate political agendas is one
effective strategy that can create a sense of closeness and exclusivity among
the population. As previously mentioned, such use of minority languages
can help bridge the communication gap between the messenger and the
receiver of the message and increase the credibility of the content. Political

parties in Malaysia, including GPS, have strategically used social media, such as Facebook, as a propaganda tool to appeal to different segments of the population, including rural communities (Rahim, 2021).

"Sarawak First" Campaign by GPS of Sarawak

One noteworthy political campaign to mention in this book that emphasizes a sense of exclusivity is the "Sarawak First" campaign launched by GPS to appeal to local voters ahead of the Sarawak state election in 2021. The campaign propagates the active role of GPS in helping Sarawak regain its rights as enshrined in the Malaysia Agreement of 1963. This campaign appealed to a significant segment of Sarawak's society due to long-standing resentment toward the federal government over the underdevelopment of Sarawak, freedom of religion issues, the protection of native customary rights, and the continuing use of English and Bahasa Malaysia as official languages of the state. The "we versus them" propaganda approach by GPS worked well, especially with the emotional political climate in Sarawak due to continuous dissatisfaction toward the federal government (West Malaysia) due to perceived manipulation of Sarawak's resources to develop by the federal government. Over the years, negative sentiment toward the federal government and peninsula Malaysia could be seen through the emergence of secessionist groups. GPS successfully developed an appealing manifesto in line with the political climate in Sarawak by prioritizing the needs of Sarawakians, rejecting Malaya-style identity politics, and focusing on protecting Sarawak's right to be recognized as a federation, not a state, in Malaysia. ""Sarawak First" narratives are shared not only on social media in various local languages but also often mentioned during on-ground lobbying by GPS leaders, leading to an increased sense of state nationalism among Sarawak people. This multi-prong approach to promote "Sarawak First" narrative resulted in a landslide win for GPS under Abang Jo. See figure 4.5.

CHAPTER SUMMARY

This chapter delves into the diverse computational propaganda tactics employed for political cyberwarfare in Malaysia. These tactics encompass a range of sophisticated methods, such as the utilization of bots during the 14th General Election (GE14), the propagation of hateful ethnoreligious rhetoric on social media platforms like TikTok during the 15th General Election (GE15), and the strategic deployment of indigenous languages in social media for information warfare.

As the practice of computational propaganda continues to evolve in Malaysia, social media remains a potent instrument for garnering public support.

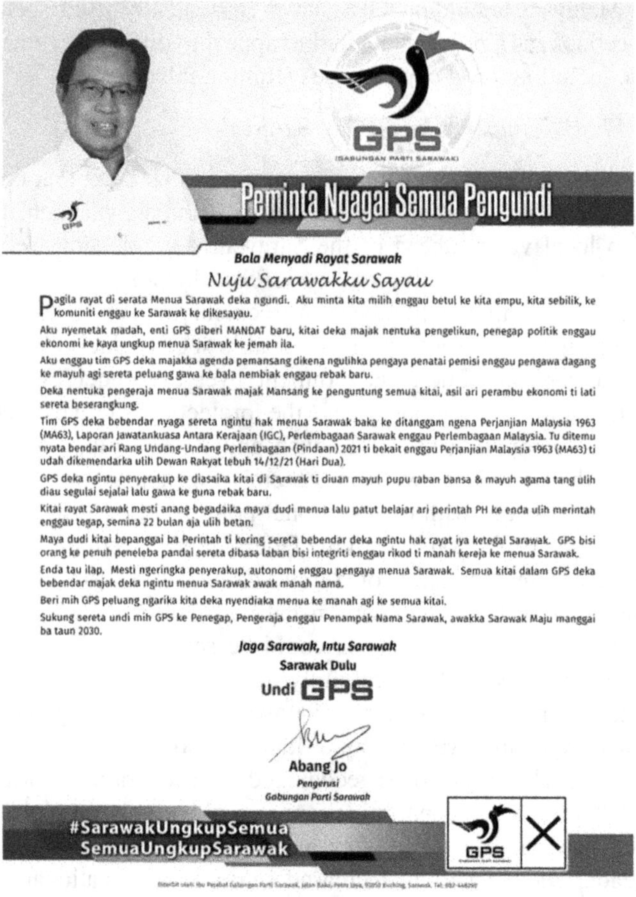

Figure 4.5   An Online Poster Was Published by Sarawak First Media, a Pro-GPS Outlet Working on Behalf of the Coalition, Featuring Abang Jo, the Chief Minister of Sarawak Malaysia and Chairman of GPS. This Poster Was Widely Shared with Multiple Facebook Groups and Pages. The Keyword "Sarawak First" Was Used to Monitor Pro-GPS Propaganda on Facebook from December 11 to 18, 2021. According to Data from CrowdTangle (2021), as Many as 799 Posts Were Uploaded on Public Facebook Pages, Groups, and Profiles Using the Keyword "Sarawak First," with 87 percent of the Content Being Pro-GPS. *Source:* Political ad, Sarawak First Media (2021).

However, the unrestrained application of computational tactics for disseminating political ideologies could jeopardize the nation's democratic health (Livingstone, 2018). Over the years, platforms such as social media have transitioned from being a casual space for connecting with family and sharing information to serving as a computational tool for social control, manipulated by savvy political consultants and exploited by politicians in both democratic and autocratic systems (Howard and Woolley, 2016).

Moreover, the ongoing advancement of technology, including AI tools and machine learning, has introduced new avenues for political manipulation. These cutting-edge technologies have the potential to constrain the digital space, thereby impeding its capacity to foster healthy public discourse and democratize information access. Consequently, it is of paramount importance to maintain vigilance and monitor the employment of such tactics, ensuring that democratic values and principles in Malaysia are preserved and upheld.

Chapter 5

Government Propaganda in Indonesia

The Burning Ambition for a Single Narrative

In this chapter, we will discuss how the Indonesian government spread propaganda on the Internet to control public opinion through the dominance of narratives in public discourse. In our extensive research on the Indonesian government's political communication since 2016, we have observed the government's attempt at constructing grand narratives bear fruition, as the state itself is now the most powerful propaganda machine in Indonesia. The government's overbearing supremacy has the power to silence dissenting opinions, control public discourse, maintain state narratives in the media ecosystem even during major political events such as the Omnibus Law protest in 2020 and the revision of Indonesia's anti-corruption law. To control public uproar over government policies, such as during the two protests, President Joko Jokowi's (Jokowi) administration deployed its propaganda machines not only to distract and disorient public's attention but also to disinform and create division among the people. Misguided and distracted citizens would then not be able to collectively find solutions to counter the state's propaganda as the government's narrative had widened the crevices of division among them. Unlike in the preceding chapters, where we described various entities and their online propaganda strategies in Malaysia and other Southeast Asian countries, this chapter is dedicated solely to discussing the Indonesian government and its propaganda tactics, which are still understudied. We will be focusing on the use of digital media, such as social media, to form a grand government-friendly narrative through novel digital propaganda programs and strategic planning.

HTI VERSUS THE GOVERNMENT AND
PERPPU CONTROVERSY IN 2017

In mid-2017, the Indonesian government officially disbanded a hardliner Islamic organization Hizbut Tahrir Indonesia (HTI). According to the Indonesian government, the organization, which was a part of an international pan-Islamist and fundamentalist political organization that actively pushed for the implementation of Sharia law globally, could threaten Indonesia's unity and the state ideology of Pancasila. HTI protested that the disbanding was unconstitutional because it was not through the judicial process, and the government used a newly signed presidential regulation in lieu of law, known as Peraturan Pemerintah Pengganti Undang-Undang (Government Regulation in Lieu of Law) or PERPPU (Sinaga, Almanar, and Setuningsih, 2017), within nine days after President Jokowi signed it. HTI, represented by its lawyer, Yusril Ihza Mahendra, a constitutional law professor and politician, went to court because they believed that PERPPU could not disband a long-established organization without judicial process. The disbandment of HTI also raised concerns among civil society organizations and scholars because it showed how the government could abuse the newly signed PERPPU to disband any other organizations, such as minority religious organizations, that the government cogitates could threaten Pancasila (Burhani, 2017).

During the court process, thousands of HTI members and sympathizers frequently rallied to protest the government in front of the courthouse, and more protested via social media platforms. Hashtags such as #HTISiapBanding (#HTIreadyToAppeal) and #AllahBersamaHTI (#GodIsWithHTI) were trending on Twitter (Cahya, 2018). At the same time, hashtags countering HTI protests were also trending, although they did not get as many retweets. HTI's disbandment and judicial reviews became hot topics on social media and on the ground. Information warfare between HTI members and the Indonesian government was constant and centralized on these two topics, although the government realized it would lose, since civil society and scholars were also against the enactment of PERPPU. See textbox 5.1.

TEXTBOX 5.1. UNDERSTANDING INDONESIA'S *PANCASILA*

Pancasila is the official philosophical foundation of the Indonesian government. It consists of five principles:

1. Ketuhanan yang Maha Esa (belief in one God)
2. Kemanusiaan yang adil dan beradab (a just and civilized humanity)
3. Persatuan Indonesia (the unity of Indonesia)

4. Kerakyatan yang dipimpin oleh hikmat kebijaksanaan dalam per-musyawaratan/perwakilan (democracy guided by the inner wisdom in the unanimity arising out of deliberation among representatives)
5. Keadilan sosial bagi seluruh rakyat Indonesia (social justice for all the people of Indonesia)

Pancasila was first articulated by Indonesia's founding president, Sukarno, and has been the guiding principle of the country's political system since its independence. The objectives of Pancasila are essential in promoting national unity, democracy, social justice, a just and civilized Indonesian society. Not only in governance, but Pancasila should also be one of the guiding philosophies in social life, particularly in decision-making and choosing actions that can affect the nation and the people.

To win the battle, Jokowi's administration needed to find the "*story*" for its digital campaign to distract public attention from the issues surrounding HTI and PERPPU. At the time of one of the key HTI trials in 2017, the government's public relations (PR) team, the Tenaga Humas Pemerintah (or THP), came up with a strategic distraction campaign called #KidsJamanNow (translated as Kids Nowadays), through dissemination of memes and posts on social media platforms showing young people's lifestyle in modern Indonesia. The hashtag gained traction in a short of period of time and became one of the trending hashtags during the HTI trial period. The objective of introducing the "story" #KidsJamanNow is straightforward—to drown out HTI and PERPPU-related hashtags and divert people from talking about the ongoing HTI trial. Through this initiative, THP successfully assisted the state to dilute public's attention to HTI and PERPPU by methodologically using government's social media channels to push for #KidsJamanNow to go viral (Idris, 2019).

THP was a group of professionals with previous extensive experience in media and communication strategies hired by Jokowi's administration as PR strategists for the government. Other than working on PR and being responsible for synchronizing government messages across ministries, their job also involved "*goreng-menggoreng isu*" (in colloquial Indonesian), which loosely translates as "stir-frying the government issues" (or making up issues). With their expertise in stirring issues, whenever crises happened, THP was often the go-to to create soft, entertaining topics and inject them on social media with attempts to make them viral. This method is often observed during political events, particularly ones that potentially put the government in a "bad light," so any criticisms aimed at the state would not seep into the news media and become public attention. This propaganda strategy, by distracting public attention to entertainment, gossip, or less threatening issues, has been used by Russia as its propaganda strategy (Bjola and Pamment, 2018) and also used by other Southeast Asian countries like Malaysia's #pulangmengundi in 2018 (see chapter 3).

In today's digital age, citizens and civil society organizations have the ability to actively advocate for public concerns. To Understand this, the government must have a presence on social media and online news platforms in order to effectively communicate with and engage with the public. The widespread use of social media and messaging applications also allows for the instantaneous dissemination of information, which means that people are exposed to a plethora of messages. If messages containing scathing criticism toward the government are not controlled and become widespread on the Internet, it could affect people's perceptions.

Bernays (1928) argued that individuals have limited ability to understand complex issues such as politics and economy, and that gap provides propagandists with chances to shape people's interpretation of them. The idea of shaping people's perceptions and manipulating public consent is certainly not novel (Benkler, Faris, and Roberts, 2018). In modern democratic societies, where ideas often compete for attention, governments have their own agencies to set and promote their agendas through public and news media. In Indonesia, this work is carried out by the Executive Office of the President and other government departments such as the Ministry of Communication and Information (Kominfo) and the Coordinating Ministry of Politics, Legal, and Security Affairs (Kemenko Polhukam). Over time, these agencies have shifted their focus from setting the government's agenda and influencing public opinion to also controlling public discussion and the narrative in the digital sphere. One of the main priorities is promoting the government's version of nationalism and Pancasila ideology (Ditjen IKP Kominfo, 2018).

A CONTEXT OF INDONESIA'S POLITICAL DYNAMICS

Apart from being the largest Southeast Asian nation with the fourth largest population worldwide, Indonesia, a model of Muslim democracy in the world (Wolfowitz, 2009; Buehler, 2009; Hackett, 2018), ranks first in terms of freedom in Southeast Asia (Puddington and Roylance, 2016). Indonesia gained its independence from the Dutch East Indies (the Netherlands) in August 1945 and subsequently experienced authoritarian rule under former President Sukarno (1950–1967) and President Soeharto (1968–1998) (Heryanto, 2004). The "Reform Era" that began in 1998 is widely considered as one of the most significant and successful political revolutions in Asia, transitioning

Indonesia into a democracy. Since then, Indonesia has consistently held elections at all levels, including presidential, municipal, and local (Winters, 2013), and this democratic system has allowed for the formation of multiple political parties with diverse ideologies (Hanan, 2012). Democracy has also positively affected Indonesia's economic growth, and based on a report by Price Waterhouse Cooper's (PWC) "The World in 2050," published in 2016, Indonesia is ranked eighth in terms of global economic growth. Additionally, the Internet economy in Indonesia is projected to reach $330 billion by 2030 (Chandra, 2021).

Since its independence in 1945, the government of the Republic of Indonesia has recognized the use of propaganda as an effective means of political communication. Specifically, PR departments within the government have utilized a "personal relationship building" approach and "subsidized" information to dominate news coverage, shape news angles, and influence language and word choices. The cultural values of harmony and collectivism have also influenced the government's strategies, such as press forums, press gatherings, annual press awards, press luncheons, gifts, and even bribery to maintain good relationships with journalists (Romano, 1999).

In Indonesia, the mass media has a long history of serving the government's agenda and fine-tuning information to align with it (McDaniel, 2002). The government has argued that the press should align news and reports with "asian values" such as respect for the authority, respect for the elderly, and collective harmony, and that having these messages out is necessary for the country's development (McDaniel, 2004). But despite the government's push for such narratives, the Indonesian press places more importance on development, social responsibility, education, and national integration than on dependence on government-provided information (Romano, 1999; Sriramesh, 2004). Albeit being considered relatively free from government pressure and ranked as "partly free" (59th out of 100) in a 2021 Freedom House report, the press still faces threats from media owners who are often leaders of political parties. Also, government institutions are plagued by corruption (96th out of 180 countries on a corruption perception index, CPI 2021 by Transparency International), and bribing journalists to write "good stories" on behalf of the government has also corrupted journalistic practices. Despite the government's promises of bureaucracy reform and greater transparency, corruption remains prevalent until today. This consequently has a negative impact on access to public information and on the government's relationship with the press.

The Propaganda Actors

Our extensive studies on the Indonesian government's political communication illustrated actors within Indonesia's digital environment involved in

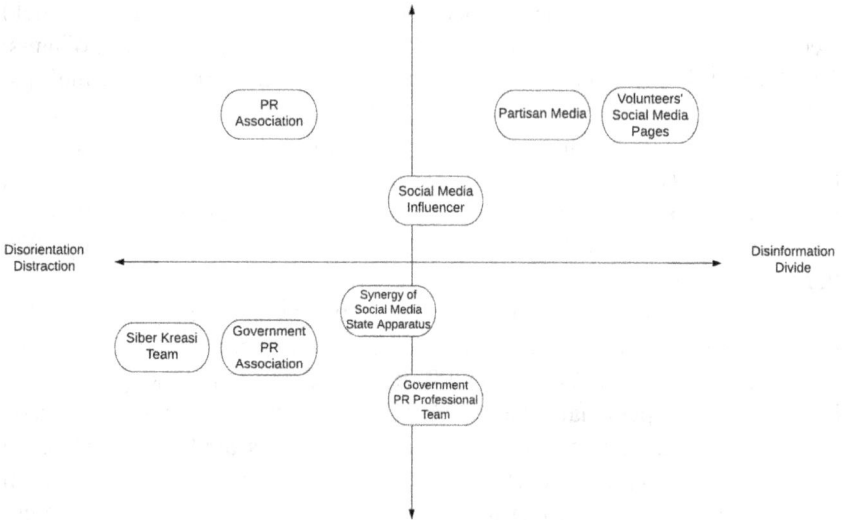

Figure 5.1 Types of Actors Involved in Supporting the Indonesian Government's Narrative on the Digital Environment. *Source:* Jalli and Idris (2023).

setting and building the government's agenda. We clustered the actors based on two categories: (1) the end means of its communication strategy and (2) the actors' position in the government (figure 5.1). In chapters 1 and 2, we identified some goals of the propagandist: to divide, disinform, disorient, and distract people. In dividing and disinforming people, the work of propagandists is not just to make people support their agendas but also to make people disconnect from their social network and go against each other. It intentionally uses any means of communication to spread a twisted version of the facts to manipulate one's opinion and behavior. Conversely, we have the lowest propaganda effect, mainly distracting or disorienting people from essential matters. A disoriented public would not be able to make a sound judgment of what is happening, and it would be even more challenging for a complex issue in politics or the economy.

The second category is the actors' position within the government. Besides the ministries and other government institutions, some actors were established or coordinated by the government. In Jokowi's first administration, the Ministry of Communication and Information (Kominfo) established around eleven information outlets to produce and publish information on government programs and policies (figure 5.2). Moreover, the ministry also established or coordinated thousands of organic cyberarmies that would help disseminate and amplify the government narrative. The troops consisted of communities, bloggers, state employees, social media task forces, and government agencies at regional and local levels. However, during Jokowi's

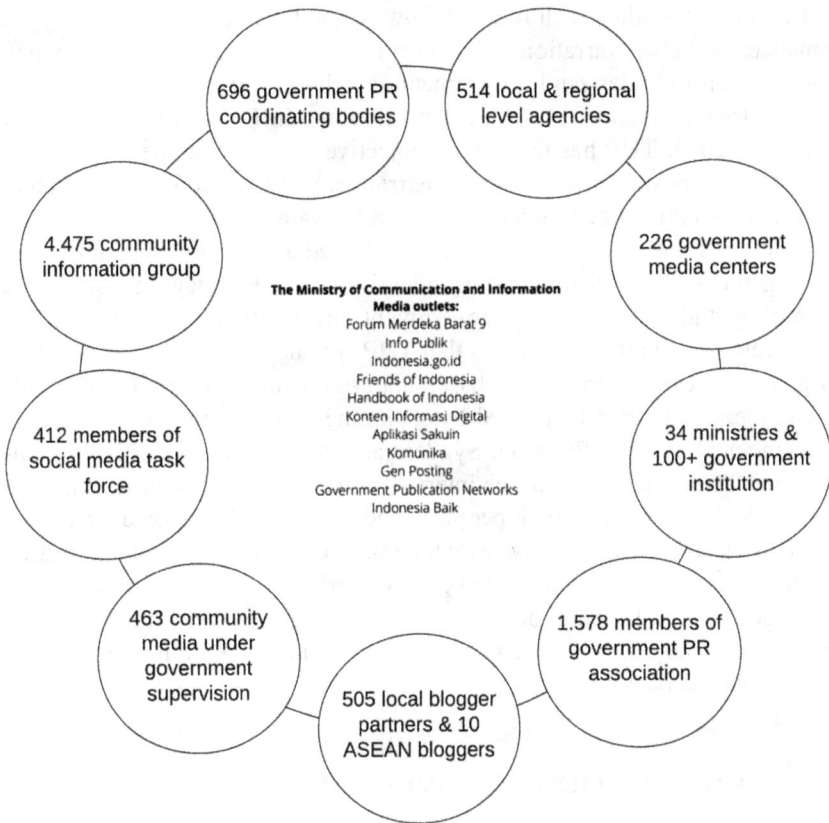

Figure 5.2 Government Information Outlets and Information Networks Are Managed by the Ministry of Communication and Information, Kominfo. *Source:* Ditjen IKP Kominfo (2018).

second period, some troops were no longer active or merged into the different government programs.

GOVERNMENT PR PERSONNEL (THP)

In 2014, after effectively using various social media platforms as communication tools, the elected president, Jokowi, commanded all government agencies, especially at the ministry level, to establish social media accounts. Jokowi's administration hired a communication professional, later given the title Government PR Personnel (Tenaga Humas Pemerintah, THP) and the establishment of THP is to ensure public communications by government agencies at the ministry's level carry Jokowi's messages and do not contradict each other. Jokowi coined the term Narasi Tunggal, translated as "One Narration." Kominfo recruited a hundred PR personnel, trained them to understand government agenda-setting, and deployed them to ministries and some government institutions. In Presidential Instruction number 9/2015, THP has three main objectives: to provide the government with data, carry out the government narrative, and disseminate government information (Priyatna, Syuderajat, and Kosawara, 2020). Their activities include monitoring and evaluating social media conversation and news, writing press releases, researching, identifying, and managing issues, and preparing and disseminating government information on social media. However, among all the activities that THP conducted, the primary role was to prepare press materials and disseminate government narration to online news, social networks facilitated by social media platforms, and groups on messenger platforms (Priyatna, Syuderajat, and Kosawara, 2020). We categorized THP as actors from the internal government body whose dominant work is to distract or disorient people as they did with HTI. However, during our interview with THP, they revealed that the work also involved heating public debates and issue management by sending well-crafted government messages to social media, or as they called it, "*goreng-menggoreng*" (stir-frying) (Idris 2019). Thus, we put some part of the circle in the right area of disinformation (see figure 5.1).

ORCHESTRATION OF GOVERNMENT PROPAGANDA

In order to counter criticism, hoaxes, terrorist ideologies, and radical ideologies on the Internet, Jokowi instructed his administration to establish a collaborative social media team consisted of teams from various government agencies in 2017. This team, called Sinergi Media Sosial Aparatur Sipil Negara (SIMAN) or the "Synergy of Social Media State Apparatus," is open to any state employee who wants to join the force to spread government narratives and counter criticism aimed at the government. *Viralisasi*, translated as going viral, was the keyword implanted on every government official's head who joined the SIMAN workshop during 2017–2019. The workshop was part of recruitment before officially joining the Indonesian government's "special forces" on social media. Milda,[1] a government officer from Bengkulu Province who participated in one of the workshops, wrote in her blog Mildaini that they learned to create memes and short videos to disseminate government narration, as both are the two forms of media that have higher chances of going viral.

SIMAN was established by the Coordinating Ministry of Political, Legal, and Security Affairs (Kemenko Pulhukam) and Kominfo and successfully recruited government officers from the ministry level, local government, state universities, and other government institutions. In 2019, around 5,946 government officers were recruited as SIMAN through 42 workshops (Kominfo, 2019). The organizational structure of SIMAN (figure 5.3) consists of a PR bureau from every ministry and government institution that will report to a coordinator from Kominfo. Later, the coordinator will report to a task force from the Coordinating Ministry of Political, Legal, and Security Affairs— which also controls the Indonesian Ministry of Defense, the Indonesian National Army, and the Indonesian National Police. At the middle level, there is a unit of analysis and production and a unit of distribution and monitoring. At the bottom level are the members of SIMAN.

The SIMAN's workflow above illustrates how SIMAN is designed to counter criticism, hoaxes, and hate speech toward the government in less than two hours. After which, the SIMAN team must work to develop counter-messages and amplify them on social media to make them viral. The workflow process in figure 5.4 show how criticism, hoaxes and hate speech are first sent to an expert team for content analysis, then passed on to a production team, a distribution team and SIMAN members whose task is to make the message go viral on social media. SIMAN members use official accounts of government agencies and their private social media accounts which makes it difficult to distinguish support for government policy from SIMAN or regular citizens. During the HTI's judicial process, Kominfo published 13 infographics to explain the importance of the new law and defend the Jokowi's newly established policy (Idris, 2019). THP and SIMAN distributed all the infographics on social media to support the government's controversial laws.

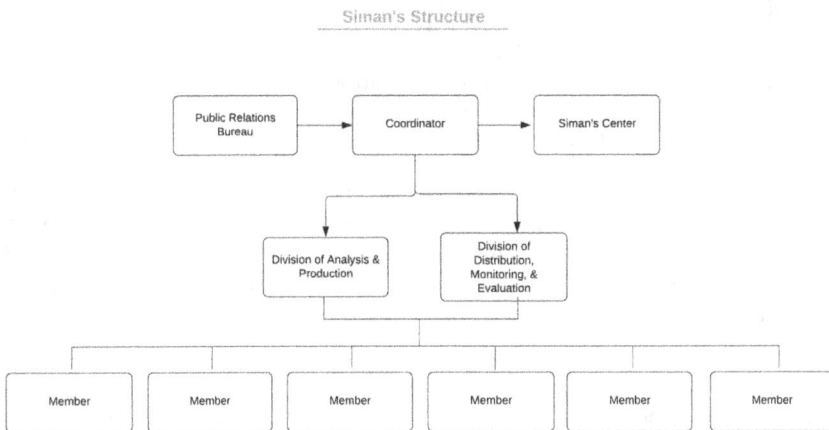

Figure 5.3 The Organizational Structure of SIMAN. *Source:* Created by the authors.

Negative Issues

Public	Siman's center	Siman's coordinator at the agency level	Siman's team members	Public

Negative Issues

Hoax & Hate Speech

Expert Team's Analysis

Distribution

Monitoring & Evaluation

Classifying Issues

Analysis & Production

To Get Viral

Public Support: Polling, Trending Topic, Media Monitoring

Within 60-100 minutes

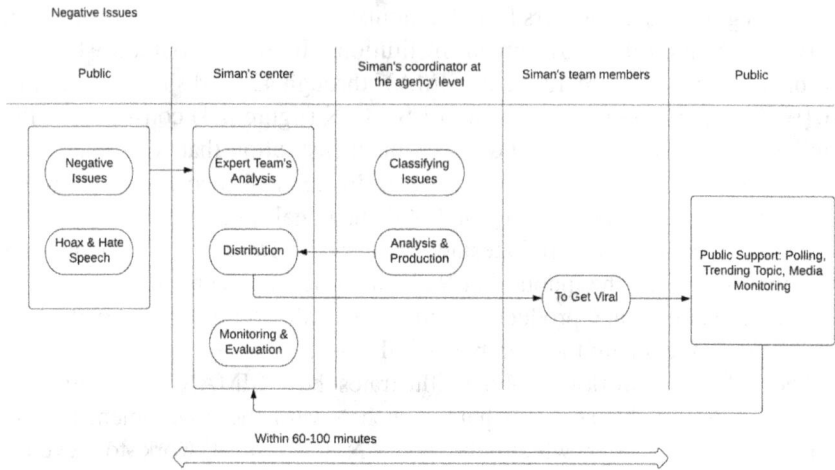

Figure 5.4   SIMAN's Workflow to Counter Negative Issues and Criticism toward the Government. *Source:* Created by the authors.

Countering public criticism toward the PERPPU was a key agenda in SIMAN's workshops (Sumari, 2018). This was in addition to the 2017 Election Law, which also drew public criticism due to its provision that allows ex-graft convicts to participate as candidates in the elections (Sapiie, 2018). There were at least three main frameworks that the Indonesian government aimed to instill in the minds of these cyberarmies during SIMAN workshops or government meetings (Kemkumham RI, 2018; Lemhanas RI, 2017; Kemkumham RI, 2019; BKN RI, 2018). The first framework is that national security is threatened by radical and terrorist groups, intolerant groups, and "haters," defined as anyone who makes negative comments and criticism toward the government, including civil society groups and academics who protested the controversial laws. The second framework is that government officials must keep social media conversations free from hoaxes, negative issues about the government, and hate speech and counter them with positive information about the government, implying that government officers must be obedient and support any government policy without any doubts. The third framework is that countering negative issues and criticism toward the government will only be successful if there is synergy among all government bodies that fully support the government's single narrative, meaning there should be no dissenting opinions or disagreements with the single narrative formed by the national government.

The orchestration of these SIMAN and THP networks was not only limited to countering criticism but also included promoting government policies and programs. In 2017, during an outbreak of diphtheria in Indonesia, SIMAN members actively sent messages and mentioned other government agencies to ensure their tweets were widely seen. In our research on social media conversation in December 2017 during the diphtheria outbreak, when the Ministry of Health urged the public to get vaccinated, the Indonesian government even declared the diphtheria outbreak as a catastrophic event (Kapoor, 2017). The hashtag #ImunisasiCegahDifteri (translated as #VaccinationPreventsDiphteria) was used as a public call for vaccination. Within a month, 3,558 tweets were collected using this hashtag (from December 2017 to January 2018). In addition to government agencies, state employees and government PR officers also sent out messages on the network.

Our study disclosed that the Ministry of Health's account (@KemenkesRI) resides at the nucleus of the communication network, channeling information to other networks in the framework of the topic ecosystem. As we mapped the network, we identified a cluster of discussions nearest to the Ministry of Health, which incorporated the hashtag #sinergimediasosialASN along with the main hashtag #ImunisasiCegahDifteri. The majority of users employing these hashtags functioned as conduits to other groupings within the network. This means that those users who included the hashtag #sinergimediasosial-ASN in their posts were most successful in transmitting information from the ministry's account to other government bodies and their individual networks.

Based on their activities, SIMAN is categorized as a part of the government body that primarily functions to distract and disorient the public. Although SIMAN serves as a force to amplify the government's narrative, the team members are not directly involved in designing and producing content. They mainly rely on coordinating bodies in the central government, such as Kominfo and the Coordinating Ministry of Political, Legal, and Security Affairs, to provide the messages. However, since they are actively involved in propagating the government's controversial policy on HTI, in figure 5.1, we have placed some of these actors in the area of disinformation and division.

CYBERARMIES: FROM VOLUNTEERS TO PROPAGANDISTS

The third group of actors we want to discuss are volunteers and partisan media. We have placed these actors on the upper right of figure 5.1 because they operate outside of the government and their primary role is to disseminate disinformation. Jokowi's populism began in 2010 when he, as the mayor of Solo City in Central Java Province, received an award as a public sector leader who supported anti-corruption (Hamid, 2014). The mass media reported that his "*blusukan*" activities, which involved visiting village and slum areas to talk with people, were an antithesis to President

Susilo Bambang Yudhoyono's leadership style, which many considered slow and not progressive (Hunt, 2010; Sihaloha, 2013; Prabowo, 2014). When Jokowi ran for the position of governor in Jakarta Province, the capital of Indonesia, many social media users and online forum influencers supported his candidacy and his running mate Basuki Purnama, also known as Ahok. The supporters, who called themselves Jasmev (Jokowi-Ahok Social Media Volunteers), worked voluntarily to spread positive information about Jokowi-Ahok and flooded online platforms during the election campaign (Suaedy, 2014). Later, Jokowi-Ahok declared that the volunteers were part of their campaign teams and provided them with social media training to win the election (Sancaya, 2012). After winning the election, Jasmev was disbanded but reactivated in 2014 when Jokowi ran for the presidential election (Rakhmani and Saraswati, 2021). In 2014, Jokowi and his running mate Jusuf Kalla, a senior politician from the Golkar party and former vice president in Yudhoyono's first term, won the election. Mass media coverage and scholars have acknowledged that his populism benefited greatly from the cyberarmies (Suaedy, 2014; Rakhmani and Saraswati, 2021; Hamid, 2014; O'Neill, 2014; Vaswani, 2014; Bollier, 2014).

The Jakarta gubernatorial and Indonesian presidential elections taught Jokowi that managing public discourse and popularity on social media is critical for his populism. Winning a close gap of 6.3 percent votes over his rival Prabowo Subianto, Jokowi faced challenges from the public, political parties in the legislature, and political opponents. In addition to forming THP in 2014 and SIMAN in 2017, Jokowi's administration invested heavily in cyberarmies, influencers, and online communities. In 2017, Indonesia Corruption Watch, an NGO that focuses on monitoring corruption in Indonesia, revealed that Jokowi's administration spent around 17.68 billion Indonesian Rupiah (equivalent to 1.2 million USD) in the government budget for social media influencers (CNN Indonesia, 2020). The amount increased to around 3.9 million USD in 2018, a year before the 2019 election.

In our research on Indonesia's 2019 presidential election, cyberarmies, fake accounts, and bots were used to amplify conversations and make them go viral (Jalli and Idris, 2019; Alizen and Fajar, 2021). The activity of cyberarmies was particularly intensive during the candidates' debates on television, as debates are major political events in the election. During these debates, both candidates deployed their cyberarmies to create viral conversations. For example, in one of the debates, Jokowi's team used the hashtag #DebatPintarJokowi (translated as intelligent debate by Jokowi). This hashtag went viral on Twitter during and after the second presidential debate and aimed to celebrate Jokowi's success in the debate. However, analysts judged that Jokowi did not address any substantial issues during the debate (Azhari and Bisara, 2019). We collected 170,069 tweets using this hashtag, in which the conversation networks consisted of 9,006 users (nodes) who sent 33,272 tweets (edges). On average, each user sent 3,694 tweets, and the networks comprised only 66 clusters. The number of clusters was relatively small for around 170,000 conversations.

The graphical representation of the network demonstrates the use of synchronized social media accounts that acted as boosters, overwhelmingly dominating the discourse network. The patterns of their interactions revealed clusters of these booster accounts, which predominantly retweeted the same messages propagated by a core account within the group (Idris, 2018). A majority of users were linked solely to the central point from which the message was disseminated and did not engage with each other or with users from different clusters. In other words, most users within these clusters solely magnified the primary messages transmitted from the major nodes. During notable political events, such as the presidential debate, public opinion must be favorable to candidates to influence news media reports. Therefore, clusters of amplifiers are needed to get critical messages viral on social media. The government's strategy of using social media influencers and online communities to promote government programs and shape public opinion has continued until today. This strategy has been used in a number of controversial issues, such as the public protests in Papua (Strick and Syavira, 2019), the establishment of the Omnibus Law on Job Creation (Idris, 2020), the revision of the Corruption Law, also known as the KPK Law (Wijayanto and Berenschot, 2021), and tourism recovery during the pandemic (CNN Indonesia, 2020). News reports indicate that social media influencers, along with cyberarmies, disinformative websites, and bots, have been successful in swaying public opinion, silencing criticism, and dividing society into pro-government and opposition groups.

In a large public protest, such as the establishment of the Omnibus Law on Job Creation, the president himself led the narrative in orchestrating the propaganda (Arbi, 2020). The law amended 79 existing laws and more than 1,200 articles, from labor and mining regulations to business licenses and environmental laws. Around ten thousand people went on strike and protested in many areas in Indonesia (Arbi, 2020), involving students, laborers, academics, and civil society organizations. They demanded that the government revoke a law that they claim would only benefit employers and investors while trampling on the interests of workers. Amnesty International Indonesia said that the law not only violated legal procedures, but its substance also had the potential to violate human rights (Amnesty, 2020).

Responding to the massive public protest against the law, Jokowi condemned that the demonstrations were triggered solely by hoaxes and disinformation. Kominfo's minister, Johnny G. Plate, amplified the message, resulting in furious criticism on social media (The Jakarta Post, 2020). The accusation, made by many civil society organizations, was an attempt to discredit the fight against the cancellation of the Job Creation Act (CNN Indonesia, 2020; Anwar, 2020).

Amid clashes between the government and protesters, our observations show that the government's strategy effectively diverted people's attention from the demonstrations. Data from CrowdTangle, a tool that records public conversations owned and operated by Facebook, showed that there were 15,819 conversations with the keyword "create work" in Indonesia a week before the president's statement. Based on the total number of interactions, such as Likes, Comments, Shares, and giving the impression of Love, Wow, Haha, Sad, Angry, and Care, the top conversations were first related to demonstrations and irregularities in the process of enacting the law. However, after Jokowi and the minister's statements, the public discussion and dominant narrative changed in favor of the government. Around 21,971 conversations on Facebook collected after the comments, the dominant discussion, showed that demonstrators did not understand the substance of the law and supported Jokowi (Idris, 2020). Social media influencers and troops amplified such topics of conversation. We also found entertainment narratives among the top posts with the highest engagement after Jokowi's accusation, such as a story about an Indonesian celebrity supporting the law and a handsome policeman during the public protest. This "entertainment" and irrelevant narrative was similar to the strategy when THP promoted the #KidsJamanNow hashtag during the judicial review of HTI's disbanding.

Jokowi's strategy of attacking public protests is an example of the gaslighting strategy that scapegoats his opponents. American philosopher and literature scholar Kenneth Burke called this long-standing rhetoric "scapegoating" (Griffin, Ledbetter, and Sparks, 2018). In its development, the technique of scapegoating the opposing party that aims to confuse the public is known as the gaslighting technique. In terms of psychology, this gaslighting technique is a strategy to attack the opponent by questioning the opponent's credibility. Psychological studies refer to gaslighting perpetrators manipulating their victims and the environment around them so that victims believe they are hallucinating and incompetent to judge something (Walzer, 2019).

In a political context, the phenomenon of using the gaslighting technique is carried out very openly and repeatedly by the president of the United States of America, Donald Trump (Sinha, 2020). This gaslighting technique is also used to maintain the racial hegemony of whites over blacks in America (Baker, 2020). When the Black Lives Matter movement took place, for example, the All Lives Matter narration also emerged, which was considered to have a hidden goal of perpetuating white hegemony (Davis and Ernst, 2016). Gaslighting in the political context is a contemporary form of propaganda because it contains elements of manipulation, a great power of persuasion, and a massive persuasion effect (Sinha, 2020). Two essential components determine the success of a gaslighting technique: disinformation and the environment that supports the narrative.

Gaslighting techniques are used by the government to cover up political promises or wrongdoing. This is achieved by conveying disinformation in a planned manner as well as haphazardly on various occasions. In the case of Indonesia, the narrative is supported by volunteers' accounts, such as Denny Siregar, the Facebook page "Info About President," and the prominent Indonesian lawyer Hotman Paris. The mass media also supports this narrative by airing news that reinforces it. Additionally, the technique takes advantage of the increasing polarization in the political climate since the 2019 presidential election, resulting in many people in Jokowi's camp fully defending his narrative.

Orchestrating the Narrative

In August 2021, the Indonesian Minister of Communication and Information, Johnny Plate, issued a press release entitled "The orchestration of public communication in handling the COVID-19 pandemic." In the statement, Johnny Plate emphasized the importance of controlled messages and communication channels, similar authoritarian approach before the era of political reform (pre-1998 revolution). He emphasized that the narrative and orchestration must be focused on the central government and the president.

> We follow the presidential system, where the president's directives and policies, the president's vision and mission are the only directions, including direction for our national development plan. (Kominfo RI, 2021)

Johnny Plate emphasized the importance of maintaining the government's narrative through public communication channels. At the time, the focus was on the government's COVID-19 response, but the goal of maintaining a single narrative extends to other priority programs and public policies, such as the Indonesian presidency in the G20 (Iprahumas, 2022), infrastructure projects (Kominfo RI, 2016), and the Omnibus Law on Job Creation and Economic Incentives (Adhrianti, 2018). One government tool used to disseminate and amplify its narrative is the "Ikatan Pranata Humas Pemerintah" (IPRAHUMAS), an association of state employees whose job is in PR. In theory, these actors should work on designing and carrying out a strategic communication approach for the government, but their roles have been diminished to become state cyberarmies, especially during important government events.

In 2022, Indonesia held the presidency of the G20 and hosted members of the 20 countries in Indonesia. To support the publication of the event and create public awareness, the Ministry of Communication and Information urged the government PR apparatus to amplify all messages related to the G20. The Director General of Information and Public Communication, Usman Kansong, a former senior journalist who was also a member of Jokowi's winning team in the 2019 election, instructed all government officials to consistently orchestrate the government's narrations. In his speech, Kansong reminded the state apparatus that the challenge of public communication today is the decentralization of authority and decision-making. As a state apparatus, government PR personnel must be able to orchestrate messages and be willing to be orchestrated (Observation, 2022).

The government instructed its PR officers to amplify its success in the G20 presidency, and incentivized participation by including it in their performance records. According to regulations set by the Ministry of Administrative and Bureaucratic Reform, efforts to support the government narrative include creating infographics, videos, vlogs, or Twitter threads, reposting them on social media platforms, and actively monitoring and clarifying hoaxes about the G20. These efforts would earn points that could later be reported as part of one's performance. Although the state PR apparatus is expected to support government programs and policies, through the incentivization of participation, the system becomes transactional, driving PR officers to increase participation mainly for personal gain. Establishing a regulation and rewarding the state apparatus with points has diminished their strategic role and turned them mainly into a government tool. The spread of positive news about the G20 by the state apparatus could mislead people on important agendas and issues of the G20. Based on their function to support the government narrative, we put this actor on the bottom left of the diagram (figure 5.1).

The press agentry or propaganda communication model recommends activities that can create publicity for or raise awareness of an organization (Grunig and Grunig, 1992). Within this model, communication is designed to follow a one-way pattern to attract public attention without the need to explain the complete process of an event, with an emphasis on positive images of the government or its officials (Water and Williams, 2011). Within the social media context, these attention-seeking activities could be understood in the form of using exciting and emotional words and exaggerated, overemphasized claims (Water and Williams, 2011).

The use of PR officials as a tool for propaganda was evident in the government's objective utilization of social media, primarily to gain public attention and present positive images. Based on these discussions, the key image the Indonesian government wanted to project was that it was working hard for its people. Social media messages emphasized the government's performance and adopted frames that reinforced the message of Jokowi effectively leading his administration, and they all had to convey a single narrative.

The role of government PR officials will be significant as a state propaganda apparatus in the coming years. At the government's Public Relations Outlook 2023 event, Kansong instructed PR officials to strengthen their networks and fully support the government in "socializing" the newly enacted 2022 criminal code (HRW, 2022). The Indonesian parliament passed the law despite public protests and criticism from academics and human rights advocates (Strangio, 2022). In addition to articles that infringe on individuals' privacy, the new law could be used as a tool by the government to criminalize citizens if they are considered to have insulted the president, vice president, government bodies, and state institutions (Lamb and Teresia, 2022). Kansong also added that government PR officials must also promote the new code to other countries, as he believed the substance of the code is fine as long as government PR can communicate the good intention of the law (YouTube Unpad, 2022).

INDONESIA CAMPAIGN TO "SPEAK WELL"

Another actor that supports the government narrative is the Indonesia Public Relations Association, or "Perhimpunan Hubungan Masyarakat Indonesia" (Perhumas). It is a professional association with members from both the private and public sectors, with around 3,000 members (Perhumas, 2017). The association's main function is to mislead people with its campaign to advocate that Indonesians should speak positively on social media, using the hashtag #IndonesiaBicaraBaik (Indonesian Speaks Well). Members of Perhumas amplify messages that a reasonable citizen should not spread criticism, hate, and hoaxes on social media and that a good citizen should only speak positively on social media. At first glance, the message may seem like promoting media literacy on social media. However, the emphasis on becoming a good and obedient citizen, whose moral value is speaking only positively on social media, could stifle criticism of the government.

Furthermore, the campaign received support from Kominfo, which has a close alliance with Perhumas. Some high-level government officials are members of the association's honorary council and advisory board (Perhumas, 2017; Perhumas, 2021). In this campaign, Perhumas also collaborated with the Ministry of State Secretariat and The Executive Office of the President (Perhumas, 2019). In one of the meetings between Perhumas and the government, the Deputy for Public Relations of the Ministry of State Secretariat, Eddy Cahyono Sugiarto, stated that the campaign to advocate for Indonesians should speak well #IndonesiaBicaraBaik had the same spirit as the government's goal of spreading optimism throughout the country. Therefore, the movement can contribute to the government's success (Perhumas, 2019).

In President Jokowi's opening remarks at Perhumas' annual national convention in 2018, he expressed his support for the campaign. Echoing the narrative that the Indonesian government is being attacked by massive negative content, provocative news, and hoaxes, Jokowi believed that the association's campaign to promote "speaking well" #IndonesiaBicaraBaik is in line with the spirit of optimism that his government carries. "If we want Indonesia to be good, if we want Indonesia to progress, we need evidence-based criticism, not deception or lies. Criticism that can educate, not a narrative that spreads pessimism and scares people," stated Jokowi in his speech (Kominfo, 2018).

As explained in chapter 1 of this book, during World War I, propaganda was utilized to not only create hatred toward the enemies but also to gain support and foster a sense of nationalism among the population (Bernays, 1928). One strategy to gain support was to use certain types of appeals (mostly emotional appeals) that could be promoted by manipulating principles familiar to the propagandist, such as the principles of gregariousness and obedience to authority (Bernays, 1928). This strategy is effectively employed by PR associations, such as the government PR Association and the Indonesia PR Association.

In his book *Rethinking Public Relations*, Moloney (2006) argues that PR can support, damage, or promote neutral attitudes toward democracy. Democracy, in its ideal form, creates a favorable condition where all entities can participate in determining what is best for society. Achieving this requires all voices to contribute to the public sphere. PRs' neutral role is "a bridge" to mediate the voices between the organization and its public (Moloney, 2006). In public discourse, not every party has an equal communication service, meaning that not all people have the skill to communicate the message in interactive and efficient ways. Therefore, those lacking communication skills and channels could be excluded from political discussion in the public sphere (Moloney, 2006).

PR activities can support democracy by providing strategies for under-represented groups to be heard by the mass media and a larger audience. However, Moloney (2006) also notes that PR can harm democracy by giving more voice to authorities and industries, serving elitist interests instead of the public interest, and reinforcing power relations in society. Instead of listening to and mediating with the public, PR ends up serving the interests of authorities. And since organizations have more resources to dominate communication channels and the public sphere, their voices will dominate the conversation. This leads to the perpetuation of power imbalances and the preservation of power relations in society.

In Indonesia, public communication activities are managed by the PR division of the government agency. Government PR divisions have played a significant role in conducting public communications since the Soekarno era in 1945, especially in distributing governmental information (Dhani, Lee and Fitch, 2015). In today's Indonesian democracy, the role of government PR divisions has become even more significant as they now serve as the primary information officer responsible for providing public information and managing government social media accounts.

For government PR, implementing two-way symmetrical communication is crucial to maintaining democracy. According to Moloney (2006), PR can make positive contributions to democracy by facilitating the participation of all stakeholders in the marketplace of ideas. He emphasizes the importance of PRs' role in providing information, particularly to those who are less heard and less informed. In a democratic society, it is the responsibility of PR professionals to ensure "equal access" and "equal participation" in the democratic process and problem-solving conversations (Spicer, 2000).

When examining the role of PR associations in amplifying the government's narrative and promoting obedience among citizens, it becomes clear that PR in Indonesia has not contributed to improving participatory communication in the new public sphere or strengthening democracy in the country. Instead, they have become the government's best allies in spreading propaganda.

GOVERNMENT-FUNDED MEDIA LITERACY
PROGRAM: SIBER KREASI

The Indonesian government has funded media literacy programs in communities and implemented the country's largest media literacy program. The primary objective of this government program is not only to educate about the dangers of misinformation but also to indirectly discourage the spread of criticism toward the government.

To address the challenges of disinformation and enhance digital competitiveness, the Indonesian government, through the Kominfo, established the national digital literacy program called *Siber Kreasi* in 2018. Although *Siber Kreasi* is a program, the team consists of personnel from the ministry, former social media volunteers from Jokowi's last election (Sihombing, 2020), and former expert staff to the minister (Kumparan, 2021). We have placed the *Siber Kreasi* program on the bottom left of the chart (figure 5.1) as it is a part of the government program, and its purpose is to serve the government's ambition to silence criticism and create a quiet public sphere.

When it was first launched, the literacy program reached 125,000 people in 350 locations (Kominfo, 2019). Later, *Siber Kreasi* was divided into digital literacy and talent scholarship programs. In 2021, the digital literacy program had reached around 12 million people through 20,000 online literacy classes. This government literacy program is the largest in the country compared to any programs offered by schools, universities, CSOs, or DigiTech companies. At the 2021 launch event, the Kominfo's minister, Johnny Plate, was confident that the literacy program would reach 50 million people by the end of Jokowi's second term (Rizkinaswara, 2021).

The areas of digital literacy that *Siber Kreasi* focuses on include digital skills, digital culture, digital safety, and ethics. The areas that specifically focus on misinformation and fake news are digital culture and ethics. The digital culture component emphasizes how to interact and socialize on digital platforms. Meanwhile, webinars related to digital ethics stress the importance of becoming an ethical netizen and are mainly focused on how to be a good citizen on the Internet (Literasi Digital, 2022).

However, critical aspects of this program have been noted as a subtle form of government intimidation toward critics and dissidents. One such aspect is the content of learning materials, particularly in the focus areas of digital ethics and digital culture. Instead of emphasizing critical thinking and the importance of ethics when interacting online, topics in digital ethics mainly serve as a subtle warning to citizens. Some examples of digital ethics topics include "fighting radicalism on the Internet," "becoming a Pancasila society on the Internet," "being polite and civilized on social media," "understanding the limits of freedom of expression," "digital literacy within a national perspective," "how to go viral without losing your morals," and "women understanding ethics." These topics carry the same narrative, which is to be obedient and civilized citizens.

The *Siber Kreasi* digital literacy program also served as a platform to "socialize" and remind citizens of the Information and Electronic Transactions Law, commonly known as UU ITE. This law has been criticized as a tool used by the government to suppress opposition and silence criticism, including the arrest of activists during conflicts in Papua (Dipa, 2019). The website *SemuaBisaKena* (loosely translated as Everyone Can Get It), which documents cases involving the UU ITE, recorded 768 cases of individuals affected by the law between 2016 and 2020.

In addition, the program mostly took the form of webinars with four to six speakers each, which is suitable for reaching a large audience, but this format limits interaction between speakers and audiences and does not foster critical thinking. *Siber Kreasi* was not designed as a learning program but rather as a government socialization program. Another issue is the exaggeration of the economic benefits of social media and digital platforms. In the digital culture component, we also observed topics such as "becoming an influencer," "earning money through social media," and "productive life

Table 5.1   Kominfo's and Kata Data Insight, Digital Literacy Status Survey; Responsible Actors to Stop Misinformation in Indonesia

Actors Perceived as Responsible for Stopping Misinformation	2021	2020
Kominfo	63%	54.8%
Citizen		45%
Indonesian National Armed Forces (TNI) & Indonesia National Police (Polri)	No data	44.7%
Media organizations	No data	22.7%
Digital platforms	No data	20.1%
President	No data	15.5%
Journalists	No data	14.6%
Local opinion leaders	No data	14.1%
State Intelligence Agency	No data	11.6%
Religious leaders	No data	9.3%

on social media" were presented, framing social media as a quick solution to people's problems without considering other factors such as social media algorithms and ads. The outcome of a literacy program such as *Siber Kreasi* is a reliance on government institutions to combat misinformation rather than individual responsibility. A 2021 national survey on Digital Literacy Status, conducted by the Kominfo and Kata Data Insight, shows that respondents believe Kominfo is the primary actor responsible for stopping the spread of hoaxes (63 percent). This number is higher than in the 2020 survey, in which 54.8 percent of respondents believed the ministry (Kominfo) played a central role. See table 5.1.

The 2020 survey also found that 45 percent of respondents believed it was the responsibility of every citizen to stop the spread of misinformation, followed by the Indonesian National Armed Forces (TNI) and Indonesia National Police (Polri) (44.7 percent), media organizations (22.7 percent), digital platforms (20.1 percent), the president (15.5 percent), journalists (14.6 percent), local opinion leaders (14.1 percent), the State Intelligence Agency (11.6 percent), and religious leaders (9.3 percent). However, the 2021 report only states the survey results regarding the number of respondents who think the Kominfo is responsible for stopping misinformation and does not provide the results for other institutions found in the 2020 survey.

Data from 2020 indicated a trend toward combating misinformation through law enforcement and improved fact-checking processes in news organizations, as well as individual efforts. However, prevention efforts through education institutions were not effective, as shown in surveys. A 2021 report only provided survey results for the government and did not include results from other organizations. Surveys from the last two years suggest that government-led literacy programs aimed at preventing misinformation are not as successful as claimed. Although the programs reach millions, fewer people are taking active steps to combat hoaxes. When asked about measures to stop the spread of scams, the most common response is to verify the accuracy of information, but this percentage has decreased from 84.1 percent in 2020 to 83.8 percent in 2021. Additionally, fewer people are reminding others about hoaxes, with the percentage dropping from 26.9 percent in 2020 to 17.9 percent in 2021. Conversely, the percentage of people who choose to ignore or delete misinformation has increased from 7.4 percent to 8.5 percent.

Digital literacy and information literacy are widespread issues that require the participation of all stakeholders. While the government plays a crucial role, it is essential for the entire community to actively engage in literacy programs. This engagement should not only be limited to attending government-led webinars but also to actively initiating, providing input, and adapting programs to the local context. Literacy programs should be designed to empower individuals and develop critical thinking skills, rather than reinforce state control over citizens.

CHAPTER SUMMARY

This chapter aims to examine the propaganda strategies employed by the Indonesian government to influence public opinion and advance its political agenda. These strategies include using official and unofficial channels at both the national and local levels within government agencies. The persistence of these tactics stems from a long-standing desire to control public opinion within a democratic context, coupled with poor public policy and a lack of effective communication competency on the part of the government.

Many scholars argue that Indonesia, like other Southeast Asian countries, has become increasingly authoritarian in recent years, despite the freedom gained through democratic reforms in 1998 (Rakhmani and Muninggar, 2021; Warburton, 2020). In the post-Soeharto era, the government no longer exerts control over public communication and propaganda through the Department of Information. However, freedom of speech and expression, as conveyed through mass and social media, is increasingly being suppressed by the government, particularly through populist leaders such as Jokowi. The advancements in technology and the widespread use of digital platforms have provided fertile ground for the government to control information and communication flow. Jokowi and his administration are determined to maintain a certain narrative and ensure that their agenda is followed, which is challenging given the presence of ministers and legislators from multiple political parties.

In this chapter, we discussed how Jokowi and his administration seek to shape public opinion and suppress dissenting voices by manipulating the social media narrative through the use of influencers, PR professionals, government officials, bots, and fake accounts. They aim to distract the public and influence their opinions in favor of government policies and programs. In cases where the government's approach benefits investors, political parties, and industries, such as the Omnibus Law, the president himself has been known to use tactics such as gaslighting to mislead the public.

NOTE

1. Milda, "Siman sinergi media sosial aparatur negara." *Mildaini* (blog), August 15, 2019, www.mildaini.com/2019/08/siman-sinergi-media-sosial-aparatur-negara.html

Chapter 6

Disinformation Narratives in Indonesia and Malaysia

In Indonesia and Malaysia, disinformation has become a significant issue in recent years, with both countries seeing an increase in the spread of false information online. Uncontrolled disinformation in the public sphere can undermine democracy by spreading misinformation and sowing confusion among the people, which consequently can lead to a lack of trust in government and institutions. For decades, disinformation campaigns in Indonesia and Malaysia have been used to target political opponents and stifle dissent. Digital media, such as social media platforms and messaging apps, allow propagandists to reach a large audience quickly and easily, and to target specific groups with tailored messages. By using algorithms and data analytics, propagandists can identify and target individuals who are likely to be receptive to certain types of messaging, and create and disseminate content that is tailored to their specific interests and concerns. One of the ways propagandists in Indonesia and Malaysia internalize local conflicts is by creating and spreading contentious narratives that can stoke fear, instill distrust toward certain groups, and amplify messages that promote division and hate. In this chapter, we look at disinformation narratives in Indonesia and Malaysia, focusing on ethnoreligious propaganda and how it influences democracy.

DISINFORMATION AND RELIGION IN INDONESIA AND MALAYSIA

As the two countries with the largest Muslim populations in Southeast Asia, religion is a sensitive issue that can easily spellbind people in both countries. An Indonesian Muslim scholar, Azyumardi Azra, argued that religion had found its way back to most countries in Asia, where development has been the focus of modernization and economic development in the continent. During the 2017 Jakarta gubernatorial election, the "212 movements" Muslim groups rallied to defend Islam from blasphemy and attacked President Widodo as anti-Islam (Arfianto, 2018). After that movement, pro-Islam and anti-Islam sentiments dominated the public discourse on many issues, from government policy and programs to COVID-19. In Malaysia, where Islamic law is registered in some state and federal governments, religion is a sensitive issue. The rise of political Islam in Malaysia raised concerns among political observers and scholars, and the constant use of ethnoreligious sentiments for political warfare can destabilize the country.

INDONESIA

In Indonesia, particularly after 2017, it is easy to find disinformation and misinformation related to religion on social media, suggesting a rise in polarization between conservative Muslim groups and nationalist groups in the country. As the largest Muslim-populated nation in the world, Indonesia frequently experiences strong religious sentiment in public discourse on politics. The Indonesian political landscape in the past decade has been influenced by two key political players, namely the current president of Indonesia, President Joko Widodo (Jokowi), who received support from liberal and pluralistic parties, and Prabowo Subianto, on the other hand, the other end of the political spectrum, the traditionalist conservative groups. In a study conducted by Rasidi and Sukmani in 2021, where they examined discourse on social media involving these two groups, they discovered that both political camps employed black propaganda, heavily based on contentious religious narratives, to smear, degrade, and attack the credibility of one another.

For example, in the early part of October 2018, Indonesia was quaked with the revelation that one of the country's most popular political scandals involving Ratna Sarumpaet, a veteran actress, as the nation gears up for the presidential election, was found to be a hoax (Souisa, 2018). Ratna Sarumpaet, who was also a human rights activist, claimed to have been beaten by three strangers as she was campaigning for President Jokowi's political archenemy, Prabowo Subianto in Bandung, West Java. A photo of Ratna's bruised face covered with bandages went viral on social media and text messaging apps, fueling further division between supporters of these two strongest presidential candidates. Local broadcasting agencies fell into the trap of Ratna's and her team's disinformation campaign, adding to the increased circulation of "fake news" across Indonesia. National TV stations, radios, and papers covered the story for days as divisive public sentiment grew stronger.

After reports of alleged coordinated attacks against his supporters and other violent incidents, Prabowo Subianto publicly called for an investigation by the national police agency into the matter. Similarly, Amien Rais, the former leader of Indonesia's House of Representatives, criticized the head of the national police agency for failing to protect citizens during the election campaign. However, it was later discovered that Ratna, whose story Prabowo had reacted to, had fabricated the attack and injuries to gain public sympathy. Ratna's story, which was initially believed to be true by Prabowo and others, had multiple inconsistencies, and she admitted to inventing the incident. Ratna claimed she was attacked at an airport in Bandung, West Java, but she was later found by the police in a Jakarta hospital where she had undergone plastic surgery, and her swollen face was a result of the procedure (Shelton and Iffah Nur Arifah, 2018).

According to Ratna, the goal is rather simplistic, to paint Joko Widodo, who was widely supported by liberals and pluralistic parties (Warburton, 2020), as someone who is willing to do anything to keep his status quo, to the extent of silencing his critics using physical brutalities and repressing political expressions in a Muslim-majority Indonesia. This tactic was expected to be proactive in amplifying Prabowo's political persona ahead of the election (as an honest and fair Muslim leader, while Jokowi, on the other hand, is a corrupt Muslim), which would strengthen the narrative of why Prabowo gained major support from many popular Muslim preachers and the conservative Islamic parties. But her staged drama did not last long. She offered a public apology after the lies were debunked and stated that her swollen face was due to a plastic surgery procedure that she went through in Jakarta (Purba, 2018). As a result of the controversy, Ratna, who was once Prabowo's campaign head, was sent to prison for two years for intentionally sharing disinformation and causing public confusion. The scandal had a significant impact on Prabowo's presidential campaign and resulted in increased distrust toward political figures entangled in the scandal.

Ratna's case is one of the most significant disinformation cases in Indonesia, as it attracted spectatorship from various national media outlets and also successfully deceived many prominent political players in Indonesia's politics. Ratna's case has since became one of the widely discussed case studies whenever the topic of disinformation is discussed in Indonesia. Like in many parts of Southeast Asia, disinformation has become one of the dominant problems in Indonesia's information sphere, especially during polling seasons.

Another example, in the constant battle to dominate political discourse in Indonesia is the active use of disinformation propaganda by cyberarmies or buzzers from both political camps (of Jokowi's and Prabowo's), which can easily be observed in Indonesia's digital domain. Through social media like Facebook, Twitter, and WhatsApp, Jokowi's supporters frequently propagated that the Muslim groups, especially those who opposed the government, were radical citizens, disloyal to Pancasila (Pancasila is the philosophical foundation of Indonesia, see chapter 5, table 5.1), and wanted to reform Indonesia into a more conservative Muslim nation by sanctioning Sharia law across states in Indonesia.

Name-calling propaganda strategy is often applied by calling Muslim groups such as "kadrun" a shortened form of "Kadal Gurun" (or spiny-tailed lizards—a reptile that inhabits the Middle East) and "kampret" (small bats) to degrade and disrepute them (Heriyanto, 2019). Meanwhile, on the other side, Prabowo's camp has *red-tagged* Jokowi as a communist, and his administration does not value Muslim clerics and stubbornly insists on acknowledging only secular values. Red-tagging is a sub-category within name-calling in propaganda that describes the act of labeling people or groups as communists or terrorists to discredit or justify aggressive action against them. Any pro-government supporters would be labeled as supporters of ulama (Islamic clerics) abusers and often attacked online with similar names (Rasidi and Sukmani, 2021).

Propaganda in the form of disinformation and intentional falsehoods is continuously shared on social media despite the absence of major political events. By consistently sharing inflammatory disinformation on social media through astroturfing (definition in chapter 1), propagandists, regardless of which camps they belong to, will be able to socialize and internalize societal conflicts (Asmolov, 2019). For Prabowo's propagandists, the daily strategic distribution of disinformation on religion to fuel hate toward Jokowi and his supporters was crucial to pre-emptively strengthen political grip in Indonesia ahead of the next presidential election. In early 2021, for example, two years ahead of the election, disinformation attacking Indonesia's Vice President Ma'aruf Amin was widely circulated in WhatsApp groups (Firdaus, 2021). A doctored screenshot of a "news article" was found in multiple WhatsApp groups containing "news" stating Vice President Ma'aruf Amin allegedly saying that selling alcohol to support the national economy is permissible in Islam. As expected, as the screenshot went viral on WhatsApp and was also cross-posted on several social media sites, it was later debunked and found to be fake, and intentionally distributed to discredit Ma'aruf Amin and eventually Jokowi's administration.

Another example of the use of religion to spread disinformation for political purposes in Indonesia is a viral Facebook post about a supposed hijab ban in schools, which was falsely attributed to Nadiem Anwar Makarim, a minister in President Jokowi's administration (Hasbullah, 2021). The post contained a picture of Nadiem Anwar Makarim with his daughter and a priest in a church, accompanied by a message claiming that the hijab ban was announced because the minister had married a Christian woman and had a Christian daughter, despite being a Muslim man himself. Nadiem, who serves as Indonesia's Minister of Education, Culture, Research, and Technology, faced significant backlash from social media users despite never making such an announcement. These examples demonstrate how propagandists can use false narratives to manipulate public opinion without having to wait for major political events, like elections, by constantly exposing the public to disinformation to socialize certain ideas in their minds.

MALAYSIA

Similar trends were also observed in Malaysia. Based on data published by the Malaysian Communications and Multimedia Commission (MCMC), in Malaysia, topics related to politics, race and religion and public health are the top topics of disinformation and misinformation, particularly on social media and texting apps (Yatid, 2019). Like Indonesia, more than 60 percent of the Malaysian population professes Islam, making Malaysia a Muslim-majority country (Department of Statistics Malaysia, 2022). In Malaysia, the resurgence of *political Islam*, in recent years, has become one of the concerns of many political observers in the country, since Malaysia, despite its Muslim-majority population, is religiously diverse. Islam has always been a significant political force among Muslim communities in the country especially in the 1970s and 1980s (Kepel, 2002; Chin Yong Liow, 2009) and took off to a higher level when Mahathir Mohammad was appointed as the third prime minister of Malaysia in 1981. In the later years, religious sentiment persisted, albeit fluctuated, and thus the current revitalization of political Islam raised concern among political observers and even the newly elected "national unity government" led by Prime Minister Anwar Ibrahim (since 2022). Despite the ups and downs of political Islam in Malaysia, it is still one of the key influencing factors during electoral seasons, justifying the "need" for certain parties to create strategic disinformation campaigns focusing on religious narratives.

Chapter 6

Political Islam, UMNO, and PAS

Political Islam, which refers to the "mobilization of Muslims for the purpose of gaining and maintain power" (Chin Yong Liow, 2004, pg. 185), remains dominant in political parties such as the United Malay National Organization (UMNO) and the Malaysian Islamic Parti (PAS). The use of religious grandiloquence in campaign messages, be it during lobbying or media crusade launched by UMNO and PAS, often attracts strong reactions from supporters and their opposition parties. UMNO often represents itself as a more progressive Muslim party compared to the conservative PAS, and PAS, on the other hand, has over the years propagated their political brand as "true" Islamic governance. Strong information warfare between

Ajaran Sesat; Rasul Melayu dan Ayah Pin adalah Ahli Umno

Oleh **Wartawan BO** · 28/05/2012   👁 3301

Nama : Abdul Kahar Ahmad
MyKad :500427105719
Nombor KP Lama : 3297747
No. Ahli: 00113339
Negeri : SELANGOR
Bahagian : GOMBAK
Cawangan :
KAMPONG KEMESAH
Status : AKTIF
Kategori : °

Tiba-tiba, Ahli Dewan Udangan Negeri (ADUN) Bukit Payong, Ustaz Mohd Nor Hamzah berkata, PAS yang meluluskan Undang-undang Islam itu ditudh oleh Umno yang tidak mahukan Islam sebagai 'Parti Ajaran Sesat'.

Figure 6.1 An Example of Disinformation Launched against UMNO. The Headline Reads "Heresy; Malay prophet and Ayah Pin are members of UMNO." PAS Propagandists Created Several Pieces of Disinformation and Uploaded Them on Various Blogs and Social Media Platforms to Influence the Public's Perception of UMNO. The Image Shown Is of Abdul Kahar Ahmad, or the Self-proclaimed Malay Prophet, Doxed by PAS Cybertrooper, Exposing His Personal Details Accompanied by an Image of UMNO Official Logo. Ayah Pin Was a Malay Cult Leader Who Founded the "Sky Kingdom" in West Malaysia. Both Controversial Cult Leaders Were Associated with UMNO in the Disinformation War Launched by PAS. *Source:* Screen captured by authors (2022).

UMNO and Islamic Party of Malaysia (PAS) over the years was well reported in Malaysian media. Name-calling propaganda serves as the main feature of their smear campaigns, with UMNO calling PAS "conservative," "extreme," or "ajaran sesat" (heresy), and PAS on the other hand, referring UMNO as "kafir" (or infidels), "immoral," "Parti Ayah Pin" (Ayah Pin's Party; Ayah Pin was a Malaysian cult leader and the founder of the Sky Kingdom), among other derogatory terms.

The use of disinformation in the propaganda warfare between UMNO and PAS is almost the norm in Malaysia's political ecosystem. For instance, in 2013, the late leader of PAS, Nik Abdul Aziz, made a statement claiming that the prayers of UMNO leaders and loyalists were not accepted by God, as the political party had blatantly rejected the true Islamic doctrine. The statement received immediate backlash from UMNO leaders, including from the former deputy prime minister, Muhyiddin Yassin, who said that the PAS leader (Nik Aziz) made an "aberrant" fatwa (*fatwa songsang*) (Bernama, 2013). See figure 6.1.

PAS AND DEMOCRATIC ACTION PARTY (DAP) DISINFORMATION WARFARE; DAP "INFIDELS" VERSUS PAS "WAHABI"

PAS Crusade against DAP

Other than PAS's constant information battles with UMNO, PAS is also known to have been in active information warfare with DAP. Similarly, as in Indonesia, the internalization and socialization of hate and extreme views toward opposing political parties is achieved through constant propaganda campaigns, even outside of the electoral seasons. PAS, with its fundamentalist view of Islamic governance, often in conflict with DAP's more secular stance on policies. With DAP being a Chinese-dominant party and PAS being a Malay-Muslim dominant party, there is a deep-seated rivalry between the two parties that is exacerbated by racial tension.

Both PAS and DAP propagandists and loyalists utilize social media effectively for information warfare. Intentional sharing of divisive images to attack each other's credibility can be found easily on social media, online blogs, and websites. Name-calling and red-tagging DAP leaders as Islamophobic (Zahid, 2022), communists (Nizam, 2022), and any parties collaborating with DAP as enemies of Islam (Malik, 2017) and communist sympathizers can be easily found on social media. Red-tagging is a sub-category of name-calling propaganda techniques commonly employed by political opponents to discredit individuals or groups. It is used to accuse those with whom one

Figure 6.2   #KamiNampak—A Grassroot Youth Group Observed Malaysian Political Climate with Aims to Flag Political Content That Could Inflame Religious Divisions in Malaysia—Flagged Several Local Politicians for Using Racial and Religious Rhetoric while Campaigning, Including PAS Politician Siti Zailah, Who Posted a Video on Facebook Days Leading to the GE15 Polling Day, Emphasizing Non-Muslims as Enemies with a Caption Stating, "Muslims are obligated to vote to ensure non-Muslims do not become leaders as they will ruin Islam." *Source:* Screenshot of Siti Zailah's official Facebook, on November 7, 2022, by one of the authors.

disagrees of being extremists or terrorists, thus implying that they cannot be trusted and should be avoided. This technique has been used to silence dissent and discredit opponents, often without any evidence to support the claims. See figure 6.2.

DAP and PAS: Clash of Ideologies

Amid the general election in November 2022, various attacks were launched on social media by the PAS against the DAP. PAS chief, Hadi Awang, accused the DAP of being a communist party, rejecting the belief in God and of having ties to Chin Peng, the former leader of the Malayan Communist Party (Chong, 2022). PAS alleged that the DAP was attempting to revive the Malayan Communist Party in Malaysia and to bring back Chin Peng's brand of communism, creating an environment of fear and chaos in the country.

The accusations made by PAS were not only rejected by the DAP but were also seen as a distraction from the party's underlying motives. In response to these allegations, DAP leaders such as Lim Guan Eng and Lim Kit Siang contended that PAS's accusations were merely a smokescreen for the party's own ulterior intentions, which were aimed at creating an environment of fear and mistrust within the Malaysian population. DAP has also strongly opposed PAS's push for an Islamic Malaysia, citing the erosion of secularism due to the allegedly extreme ethnoreligious rhetoric promoted by PAS (Sulaiman, 2022). DAP has argued that any attempt to implement an Islamic government in the country would be in direct violation of the Rukun Negara (National Principles), the first principle of which is to believe in God, and the Constitution, which states Islam is the official religion. In 2022, the DAP chief in Perak state, Nga Kor Ming, warned Malaysians of a potential Taliban-style government if Perikatan Nasional (PN, National Alliance, with PAS being one of the forming parties) were to gain power. He stated that Malaysia could become like Afghanistan, and such a government would allow for encroachment on the rights of the non-Muslims (Free Malaysia Today, 2022).

The differences between the DAP and PAS, which are composed of different demographic backgrounds, have further polarized Malaysians. In response to DAP's criticism of the party, PAS accused DAP of being anti-Islamic and of attempting to destroy the vital role of Islam in Malaysian society. PAS also alleged that DAP was conspiring to destabilize the country and its social fabric by attempting to undermine the very foundations of Islamic teachings and values. This ongoing clash has caused an uproar among Malaysians, with PAS loyalists calling DAP anti-Islam, and DAP supporters would call PAS extremists.

As briefly discussed in chapter 4, in the 2022 general election in Malaysia, social media was once again used as a platform for hate speech between opposing groups. This put the Malaysian government on high alert during the November election. Trending hashtags such as #13Mei, #13Mei1969, and #BangsaMelayu, which refers to the Malay race, were prevalent on Malaysian TikTok, with various content generated by neo ultranationalists and alleged cybertroopers of the PN to incite a "race war" against the Chinese community. On November 20, Malaysia saw its first-ever hung parliament, as neither of the major parties received enough votes to form a new government. There were fears that if the election resulted in a victory for Pakatan Harapan (Hope Alliance), there could be street "wars" against the Chinese. In response to the widespread #13Mei content on TikTok, Malaysian authorities reached out to ByteDance, TikTok's parent company, to monitor hate speech and disinformation on its platform. However, there were allegations that TikTok did not respond quickly enough, particularly with highly emotive content

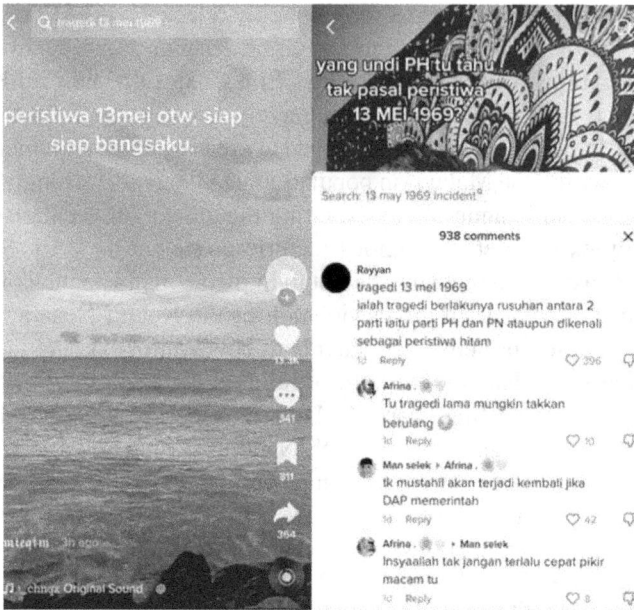

Figure 6.3 Screenshots from TikTok Videos Posted on November 20, 2022, a Day After Malaysia's 15th General Election, Featuring Content Related to the "13 Mei" Incident. The TikTok Screenshot on the Left Displays the Text "Peristiwa 13mei, siap sedia bangsaku" Written in Malay, Meaning "13 Mei incident, get ready my people/race." On the Right, Comments Are Exchanged between Users, with Two of the Comments Reading, "tu tragedi lama mungkin takkan berulang," Meaning "that's an old tragedy, it likely won't happen again," to Which Another User Responded, "tak mustahil akan terjadi kalau DAP memerintah," Meaning "it's not impossible to happen [again] if DAP governs." *Source:* Screenshot by authors.

remaining on the platform despite being flagged by users several times. See figure 6.3.

The clash of ideologies between DAP and PAS has been a long-standing issue in Malaysia, and it seems unlikely that the two parties will come to an agreement anytime soon. This clash of ideologies and active disinformation and propaganda campaigns launched by both camps have created a great deal of tension in Malaysia, deepening existing divisions and exacerbating the already fractured nature of the state.

ON HALAL

Outside the political realm, daily disinformation about religion is prevalent, targeting various aspects of religion such as the halal status of food and drink or other Muslim-related lifestyle issues. For example, a disinformation campaign on halal food was not only spread by members of the religious community, but also by business competitors. Halal certification of food products provides assurance to Muslims that the food has been prepared in accordance with Islamic law and is safe for consumption. This assurance is crucial for Muslims who want to ensure that their food and drink are in line with their religious beliefs. In 2017, a disinformation campaign aimed at the global fast-food chain Kentucky Fried Chicken (KFC) and wheat flour was launched in Malaysia (Sebenarnya, 2017). The campaign aimed to sow confusion among Muslims and cast doubt on the authenticity of the halal certification of KFC and the wheat flour used in KFC's recipes. The disinformation spread widely on social media and WhatsApp, prompting some segments of Muslim communities in Malaysia to boycott KFC. The effects of such campaigns can be far-reaching and long-lasting, as demonstrated by a study on fake news related to halal food (Moidin, Ismail, Wong, Harun, and Mamat, 2021). This study revealed that even topics regarding halal food can trigger racial and religious sentiment in Malaysia. This is especially true in the post-colonial era of Malaysia, where the Malay ethnic group and Muslims have been the dominant force in the public domain, thus anything that relates to Islam has been treated as a sensitive issue (Radue, 2019). In a study exploring disinformation campaigns during election periods in Malaysia and Indonesia, cyber-troopers highlighted that creating false narratives about religion will always elicit strong reactions from the public.

RELIGION AND GEOPOLITICAL SECURITY

Geopolitical security involves the efforts and strategies employed by nations and international organizations to protect their national interests, sovereignty, and territorial integrity from various external threats, including military aggression, terrorism, and cyber-attacks. The field encompasses the study and management of political, economic, and strategic factors that impact a country's or region's security. Geopolitical security also encompasses the relationships and interactions between nations and their influence on regional and global stability. It involves the creation and implementation of policies, strategies, and actions to tackle security challenges and sustain peace and stability. The field of geopolitical security is intricate and continuously evolving, shaped by technological advancements, geopolitical shifts, and changing threats. Malaysia and Indonesia have both confronted the task of countering disinformation concerning geopolitical security issues, such as those relating to Muslims in Palestine and Myanmar.

Figure 6.4 An Instance of Disinformation Circulating in Indonesia Concerning the Rohingya Conflict in Myanmar Was Highlighted. Numerous Posts Featured Disingenuous Headlines, Such as "Myanmar monks will make Indonesians end up like Muslims in their country," in an Attempt to Provoke Anger and Elicit Strong Reactions from Online Users. *Source:* Screenshot by authors.

There have been instances of disinformation spread by Myanmar monks in Malaysia and Indonesia regarding the situation of the Rohingya Muslim minority in Myanmar (Auethavornpipat, 2021). The disinformation campaigns have targeted the local Muslim populations, aiming to spread false narratives and manipulate public opinion. Some of the disinformation campaigns include spreading fake news on social media, such as fabricated images and videos of alleged atrocities committed by the Rohingya against Buddhists in Myanmar. There have also been reports of extremist Buddhist monks from Myanmar visiting Malaysia and Indonesia to deliver hate speeches against the Rohingya and other Muslim groups. The dissemination of such disinformation was found to be primarily perpetrated by fake accounts. One striking example was a post that featured a photo of Myanmar monks marching, with a caption that warned that "Myanmar monks will make Indonesians end up like Muslims in their country" (see figure 6.4). The post swiftly stirred up an angry response from Facebook users, with many declaring that they were prepared to go to war to fight against Myanmar. The dissemination of such disinformation can have grave consequences, as it fuels hate, violence, and intolerance between different ethnic and religious groups within a country. It can also potentially damage diplomatic relationships between nations. The dangerous consequences of disinformation were evident in the example cited above, where the provocative post stirred up angry sentiments and even the threat of violence between Indonesians and Myanmar people.

PRO-PALESTINE AND "AGENDA YAHUDI" (JEWISH AGENDA) IN MALAYSIA AND INDONESIA

Both Malaysia and Indonesia share a widespread sentiment in support of Palestine. While advocating for the Palestinian cause is a legitimate political stance, it is important to note that this sentiment can sometimes lead to anti-Semitic beliefs and attitudes. When anti-Israel sentiment is expressed in a way that targets Jews as a group rather than specific Israeli policies or actions, it can be associated with anti-Semitism. Unfortunately, in Malaysia and Indonesia, pro-Palestine activism can sometimes be accompanied by anti-Semitic rhetoric, conspiracy theories, and symbols. This is a cause for concern, as anti-Semitism, including false beliefs about a supposed "Jewish Agenda," has a long history of promoting hate and violence toward Jews.

This "Agenda Yahudi" conspiracy theory alleges that Jews are secretly orchestrating world events and manipulating international institutions to further their own interests at the expense of others. The term "Agenda Yahudi" has been used as a catch-all for various conspiracy theories, ranging from global economic control to media manipulation and even the supposed engineering of social and political unrest (Alatas, 2020). Anti-Jewish rhetoric is observable in the public sphere of Malaysia, with some political and religious leaders making propagative statements that have caused confusion among the general public, leading them to conflate all Jews with Zionists. The prevailing sentiment is that Israel is a country guilty of war crimes, and Jews are in some way implicated in these crimes. Given that almost two-thirds of the population in Malaysia is Muslim and there are very few Jewish residents, if any, the presence of anti-Semitism is a noteworthy phenomenon. This form of prejudice is mainly directed at outsiders (Alatas, 2020). During the former prime minister Mahathir Mohammad administration (first tenure, 1981–2003), Malaysia was frequently thrust into the spotlight for its stance on Israel and Jews (Simon, 2004). The Malaysian government views the injustices of the Arab-Israeli conflict through the prism of "Islamic solidarity" (Alatas, 2020).

Israel, Jews, and Zionism are often grouped together as a common enemy of Islam, with little distinction made between these three categories. This lack of differentiation serves as a form of political expediency in Malaysia, where politicians gain political mileage by denouncing Israel and Jews.

Similarly, in Indonesia, anti-Semitic sentiments have been observed in various forms, including cartoons in newspapers and magazines as well as social media posts. One notable example occurred in 2016, when an Indonesian artist for Marvel Comics was fired amid global outcry after his illustrations were revealed to contain hidden anti-Semitic references (Shepherd, 2017). Social media has also played a significant role in the dissemination of anti-Semitic content in both countries. With the rise of social media platforms such as Facebook, Twitter, and WhatsApp, disinformation can spread quickly and easily, often without any critical analysis or fact-checking. Online forums, chat rooms, and social media groups dedicated to the pro-Palestine cause can sometimes become echo chambers for anti-Semitic rhetoric and disinformation. This can lead to the further entrenchment of such beliefs among followers, potentially leading to the normalization of anti-Semitic attitudes.

Anti-Semitic disinformation in the region also extends to religious institutions. In some instances, mosques and religious gatherings have been platforms for disseminating conspiracy theories and anti-Jewish sentiments. For example, in 2018, a religious gathering in Indonesia featured a preacher who claimed that the deadly tsunami in Indonesia was a punishment from God because of the government's support for Israel. By connecting natural disasters to the "Jewish Agenda," such narratives perpetuate unfounded beliefs about Jewish control and manipulation of world events. The conflation of anti-Israel sentiment with anti-Semitic rhetoric poses a risk to the Jewish communities in Malaysia and Indonesia (Alatas, 2020; Ali, 2010). While the number of Jews residing in these countries is relatively small, the presence of anti-Semitic attitudes can still have a significant impact on their safety and well-being. Moreover, the normalization of anti-Semitic rhetoric can contribute to a broader climate of intolerance and discrimination against other minority groups in the region.

Anti-Semitism is widespread in Indonesia and is often linked to hostility toward the country's Chinese minority, who are frequently compared to Jews (Smith, 2018). Scholars and journalists have drawn comparisons between anti-Semitism in Europe and anti-Chinese prejudice in Southeast Asia, and these analyses reveal that, akin to Jews in the twentieth-century Europe, Chinese communities in the region have been unjustly blamed for various issues, including being labeled as both communists and capitalists, and have been subjected to several instances of large-scale violence (Ainslie, 2023; Reid,

2010; Goldman, 1999). Similarly, in Malaysia, Chinese leaders are frequently associated with the term "Yahudi" (Jew) due to the portrayal of both groups as capitalists who pose a threat to the rights and national security of native Malaysians. However, there is no historical or cultural connection between Jews and the Chinese in Malaysia, and the linking of the two groups is based on unfounded and baseless claims (Reid, 2010).

Sinophobia in Indonesia and Malaysia

Indonesia Chinese Economic Domination and Communist Rhetoric

During the pandemic, anti-China sentiment intensified worldwide, particularly in countries like Indonesia and Malaysia (Rich, 2020). Historically, Indonesia experienced two significant anti-China clashes: one in the 1960s, when thousands of ethnic Chinese were suspected of being communists and killed during a revolution, and another in the 1998 reform era, when hundreds of Chinese people were blamed for the country's financial crisis and lost their lives (Rakhmat and Aryansyah, 2020).

Before the pandemic, disinformation in Indonesia mainly focused on the presence of unlawful Chinese migrants. The spread of false information led to further unrest among Indonesians, especially the local population, who believed that Chinese workers were stealing their job opportunities (Suryadianata, 2020). In 2018, for example, disinformation circulated through WhatsApp groups claimed that Chinese workers had fired at innocent people on the streets. This story aimed to reinforce the idea that China was colonizing Indonesia by sending its workers to the country and used a "crying loudly" emoticon to provoke emotional reactions. See figure 6.5.

Alongside the narrative of Chinese economic dominance, disinformation about the spread of Chinese communist ideology also gained traction. In 2018, one of the most widely shared Facebook posts, according to CrowdTangle data, featured a purported invasion by the Chinese Red Army disguised as workers on a light rail transit project between Indonesia and China. Over 63,000 accounts shared the post, eliciting predominantly angry and shocked reactions. Eventually, Indonesian police arrested several individuals, including a street food vendor, for spreading disinformation about Chinese workers in various regions of Indonesia (CNN Indonesia, 2019; Tim Merdeka, 2019). See figure 6.6.

The onset of the pandemic shifted sentiments and disinformation from the topic of illegal Chinese workers to portraying China as the virus's origin and a malevolent force. In our study examining COVID-19 stigmatization

Figure 6.5   Disinformation Circulated in a WhatsApp Group Claiming that the Chinese Are Colonizing Indonesia with Illegal Workers Who Act Recklessly. *Source:* Indonesian Hoaxes Facebook Page (2018).

on Twitter conversations using the keywords "corona" and "covid," we found that stigmas in both Malaysia and Indonesia frequently involved using "China" or "Chinese" to describe the disease (Idris et al., 2022). Our findings also revealed a strong tendency to assign blame to others. In Indonesia, the primary stigma revolved around attributing the pandemic to China and the Chinese community. This widespread sentiment was fueled by the Indonesian government's policy of allowing Chinese tourists and foreign workers into the country, despite increasing COVID-19 cases worldwide. As a result, discussions about COVID-19 in Indonesia expanded beyond its medical aspects and often incorporated political viewpoints.

"CINA PENDATANG" NARRATIVE IN MALAYSIA

"Cina pendatang" is a derogatory term used to refer to Chinese immigrants in Malaysia. It is a narrative that portrays the Chinese as foreigners who have come to Malaysia to take advantage of its resources and opportunities without any intention of assimilating into the local culture. The "Cina pendatang" narrative emerged during the British colonial era as a way to create divisions

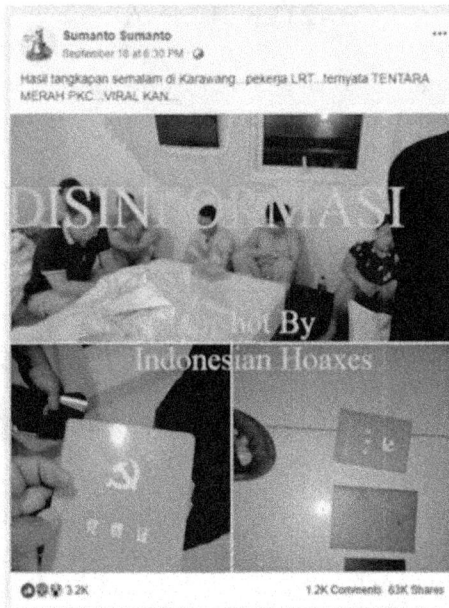

Figure 6.6 Depiction of a Disinformation Campaign that Circulated on a WhatsApp Group, Claiming that the Chinese Red Army Had Entered Indonesia Under the Guise of Construction Workers. This False Narrative Was Debunked by the Indonesian Hoaxes Facebook Page in 2018. *Source:* Screenshot by authors, from Facebook.

between different ethnic groups and maintain colonial control. The British favored a divide-and-rule approach, classifying the population based on their ethnicity and assigning specific roles to each community. The Chinese were predominantly involved in mining, trade, and commerce, which led to the stereotype of the Chinese as opportunistic, untrustworthy, and unwilling to integrate with the local population. This narrative has been used to justify discrimination and prejudice against the Chinese community in Malaysia and has contributed to the creation of an environment of tension and mistrust between different ethnic groups in the country (Albury, 2021). During Malaysia's 15th general election in 2022, the "Cina pendatang" narrative was widespread on social media platforms such as TikTok. There were numerous allegations that Chinese leaders were attempting to deprive Malay people of their rights by advocating for communism and embracing China's ideology (Jalli, 2023). The Chinese community in Malaysia has a long history of settlement and has made significant contributions to the country's economy and cultural diversity. Despite this, the negative narrative continues to be perpetuated on social media and other digital platforms, creating divisions and hindering the development of a harmonious and inclusive society in Malaysia.

CHAPTER SUMMARY

Disinformation narratives serve as a means for individuals to interpret and understand their world through "symbolic actions," as Fisher described, that possess sequential meaning (Griffin, Ledbetter, and Sparks, 2019). These narratives form part of people's identities within society, generally following a pattern of beginning, middle, and end, as suggested by Aristotle's narrative framing of settings, disruption, and resolution (Alleyene, 2015). Storytellers filter narratives through their conceptual frameworks, emphasizing the main messages or perspectives. Recognizing disinformation narratives can help address societal issues, identify potential threats, and enable proactive countermeasures. Moreover, understanding the role narratives play in shaping government policies is crucial in Indonesia and Malaysia when dealing with disinformation.

At least three primary disinformation narratives emerge from the cases examined. The first pertains to the polarization of Malaysia and Indonesia's socio-political landscape. In Indonesia, polarization initially revolved around pro- and anti-government factions, evolving into a divide between pro-Islam and pro-nationalism/state ideology (Pancasila). In Malaysia, disinformation often focuses on information warfare between political parties such as PAS and DAP during elections.

The second narrative concerns Islam as the majority religion in both Indonesia and Malaysia. This framing emphasizes perceived attacks on Islam at national and global levels, as seen in Myanmar and Palestine. Conservative Islamic groups dominate public discourse in both countries, impacting not only elections but also daily life. In Indonesia, the primary message centers on implementing Islamic values in formal settings and the belief that the government mistreats vocal religious leaders by requiring preaching certification (Michella, 2021). In Malaysia, narratives of Islam and Malaysian identity are reinforced through popular culture, including nasyid pop songs, headscarves as a standard Malaysian identity, and advocating for sharia law (Saat and Alatas, 2022). Disinformation narratives about religious issues in Malaysia and Indonesia remain prevalent, as political actors know that such discourse can provoke strong public reactions. Topics like halal certification, the Rohingya crisis, and conspiracy theories about a Jewish agenda are among the top subjects used to stir strong reactions in these Muslim-majority countries.

The third disinformation narrative revolves around Chinese domination in Indonesia and Malaysia, driven by Sinophobia. In Indonesia, historical anti-China conflicts have contributed to ongoing mistrust of the Chinese community. Disinformation narratives related to this topic include stories of Chinese economic dominance and communist rhetoric. The pandemic shifted disinformation sentiments from illegal Chinese workers to China being portrayed as the origin of the virus and a malevolent force. In Malaysia, the "Cina pendatang" narrative depicts Chinese people as foreigners exploiting resources, leading to discrimination and tensions. During Malaysia's 15th general election in 2022, this narrative was widespread on social media platforms, with allegations that Chinese leaders were attempting to deprive Malay people of their rights by advocating for communism and embracing China's ideology. These narratives hinder the development of a harmonious and inclusive society in both countries.

In conclusion, disinformation poses a pervasive threat to democracy by fueling divisions, mistrust, and prejudice within societies. By manipulating public opinion and exploiting existing tensions, disinformation campaigns undermine the principles of informed decision-making, transparency, and accountability essential for a healthy democratic system.

Bibliography

Abbott, Jason. "Vanquishing Banquo's Ghost: The Anwar Ibrahim Affair and Its Impact on Malaysian Politics." *Asian Studies Review* 25, no. 3 (2001): 285–308.

Abdul Hamid, Ahmad Fauzi. "Islamist Violence in Malaysia: Reflections from the Pre-gwot Era with Special References to the Memali and Al-Maunah Cases." In *SEARCCT's Selection of Articles*, edited by Chuah Teong Ban, 05–24. Kuala Lumpur: Southeast Asia Regional Centre for Counter-Terrorism (SEARCCT), 2020.

Acharya, Arabinda. "The Bali Bombings: Impact on Indonesia and Southeast Asia." *Center for Eurasian Policy Occasional Research Paper, Series II (Islamism in Southeast Asia)* 2 (2006): 1–5.

Adhrianti, Lisa. "Infografis penguatan reputasi kehumasan pemerintah melalui narasi tunggal sosialisasi paket kebijakan ekonomi." *Jurnal Aspikom* 3, no. 5 (2018): 1015–30.

Adjie, Moch Fiqih Prawira. "'Unhealthy in a Democracy': Concerns Mount Over Govt Using Influencers to Promote Policies." *The Jakarta Post*, August 21, 2020. www.thejakartapost.com/news/2020/08/21/unhealthy-in-a-democracy-concerns -mount-over-govt-using-influencers-to-promote-policies.html.

Adyatama, Egi, and Eko Ari Wibowo. "Kakak sepupu Jokowi disebut jadi coordinator influencer untuk pemerintah." *Tempo*, August 31, 2020. nasional.tempo.co/read/13 81124/kakak-sepupu-jokowi-disebut-jadi-koordinator-influencer-untuk-pemerin tah.

Afifah, Wida Hana, Atiqa Sabardila, and Wahyudi, Agus Budi. "Directive and Assertive Speech in Habibie & Ainun 3 Film and Its Relevance to Learning Indonesian." In *International Conference of Learning on Advance Education (ICOLAE 2021)*, 477–88. Atlantis Press, 2022.

Agate, Samantha. "19-Year-Old Killed Himself Live On TikTok — Why Aren't More People Talking About It?" *Talentrecap.com*, January 12, 2021. talentrecap .com/19-year-old-killed-himself-live-on-tiktok-why-arent-more-people-talking-ab out-it/.

Agustin, Dwina. "Ini 7 rangkaian aksi bela Islam sebelum Ahok divonis 2 tahun penjara." *Republika*, May 10, 2017. www.republika.co.id/berita/opp5r4330/ini-7 -rangkaian-aksi-bela-islam-sebelum-ahok-divonis-2-tahun-penjara.

Ainslie, Mary J. "Introduction: Judaism and Anti-Semitism in Southeast Asia and Malaysia." *Anti-Semitism in Contemporary Malaysia: Malay Nationalism, Philosemitism and Pro-Israel Expressions* (2019): 1–29.

Akami, Tomoko. "Japan's News Empire and the Domei News Agency in Occupied Southeast Asia, 1942–45." (2015).

Alatas, Syed Imad. "Islamic Attitudes Towards Israel and Jews: A Comparison of Malaysia and Indonesia." *Asia-Pacific Social Science Review* 20, no. 3 (2020): 153–62.

Albury, Nathan John. "Forging and Negating Diasporic Linguistic Citizenship in Ethnocratic Malaysia." *Lingua* 263 (2021): 102629.

Ali, Muhamad. "'They Are Not All Alike' Indonesian Muslim Intellectuals' Perception of Judaism and Jews." *Indonesia and the Malay World* 38, no. 112 (2010): 329–47.

Alizen, Ali Nur, and Maarif Setiadi Fajar. "Election Campaigns and Cyber Troops." *Inside Indonesia*. October 13, 2021. www.insideindonesia.org/election-campaigns -and-cyber-troops.

Allcott, Hunt, and Matthew Gentzkow. "Social Media and Fake News in the 2016 Election." *Journal of Economic Perspectives* 31, no. 2 (2017): 211–36. DOI: 10.1257/jep.31.2.211.

Alleyne, Brian. *Narrative Networks: Storied Approaches in a Digital Age.* London: Sage, 2015.

Ananthalaksmi, A. "Analysis: Gains for Malaysia's Hardline Islamist Party a Challenge for New PM Anwar." *Reuters*, November 25, 22. www.reuters.com /world/asia-pacific/gains-malaysias-hardline-islamist-party-challenge-new-pm -anwar-2022–11–25/.

Andre, Virginie. "'Neojihadism'and YouTube: Patani Militant Propaganda Dissemination and Radicalization." *Asian Security* 8, no. 1 (2012): 27–53.

Anwar, Muhammad Choirul. "Tolak omnibus law, buruh desak Jokowi cabut dengan Perppu." *CNBC Indonesia*. October 12, 2020. www.cnbcindonesia.com/news /20201012165232–4–193743/tolak-omnibus-law-buruh-desak-jokowi-cabut-de ngan-perppu.

Anwar, Zafira Syamim, and Nuurrianti Jalli. "Wahyu dah kurang: Journalism Practice Among Journalists in Malaysian Mainstream Media Agencies During Pakatan Harapan Tenure." *Journal of Media and Information Warfare (JMIW)* 13, no. 2 (2020): 17–30.

Arbi, Ivany Atina. "Jokowi Dismisses Criticism of Omnibus Law as Hoax News." *The Jakarta Post*, October 9, 2020. www.thejakartapost.com/news/2020/10/09/ jokowi-dismisses-criticism-of-omnibus-jobs-law-as-hoax-news.html.

Arifianto, Alexander R. "Conservative Turn Will Continue in Indonesian Presidential Election Next Year." *The Conversation*, August 13, 2018. theconversation.com/ conservative-turn-will-continue-in-indonesian-presidential-election-next-year-10 1032.

Armstrong, Hamilton Fish. "The Troubled Birth of Malaysia." In *South East Asia*, pp. 309–26. Routledge, 2021.

Article19. "Malaysia: Repeal 'Fake News' Emergency Ordinance". Article19, March 15, 2021. www.article19.org/resources/malaysia-fake-news-ordinance/.

Ashurst. "Indonesia's Omnibus Law: A Breakthrough." Accessed December 17, 2021. www.ashurst.com/en/news-and-insights/legal-updates/indonesias-omnibus -law--a-breakthrough/.

Asmara, Chandra Gian. "Jokowi and Luhut sebut corona tak kuat di cuaca panas Indonesia." *CNBC Indonesia*, April 02, 2020. www.cnbcindonesia.com/news /20200402182202–4–149466/jokowi-luhut-sebut-corona-tak-kuat-di-cuaca-panas- indonesia.

Asmolov, Gregory. "The Effect of Participatory Propaganda: From Socialization to Internalization of Conflicts." *Journal of Design and Science* 6 (2019). DOI: 10.21428/7808da6b.833c9940.

Auethavornpipat, Ruji. "Hate Speech and Incitement in Malaysia." *Preventing Hate Speech, Incitement, and Discrimination: Lessons on Promoting Tolerance and Respect for Diversity in the Asia Pacific* (2021): 119–58.

Azyumardi, Azra. "Many Asian Nations Are Experiencing a Revival of Religion in Public and Political Life." *Melbourne Asia Review*, June 6, 2022. melbourneasiare view.edu.au/many-asian-nations-are-experiencing-a-revival-of-religion-in-public- and-political-life/.

Azyumardi, Azra. "Regresi demokrasi dan resentralisasi." *Republika*, July 7, 2022. www.republika.co.id/berita/remfx2025000/regresi-demokrasi-dan-resentralisasi-1.

Baker, Paxton K. "Why Saying 'All Lives Matter' Misses the Big Picture." *CNN*, June 23, 2020. edition.cnn.com/2020/06/23/opinions/all-lives-matter-misses-the-b ig-picture-baker/index.html

Baker-White, Emily. "TikTok's Secret 'Heating' Button Can Make Anyone Go Viral." *Forbes*, January 20, 2023. www.forbes.com/sites/emilybaker-white/2023 /01/20/tiktoks-secret-heating-button-can-make-anyone-go-viral/?utm_source =ForbesMainFacebook&utm_campaign=socialflowForbesMainFB&utm_medium =social&fbclid=IwAR0DwawDMui0kIBPEtBRgL1xBuvOYoSuaBl-vC3MXPJ JZRv4qSNYFMnNn9Y&sh=498a5dd96bfd.

Bakhshi, Uday. "Indonesia and the Papua Issue: Resolution Increasingly Unlikely." *The Diplomat*, November 30, 2021. thediplomat.com/2021/11/indonesia-and-the -papua-issue-resolution-increasingly-unlikely/.

Barahamin, Andre, and Amy Chew. "Indonesia Riots: Prabowo Subianto Tells Supporters to Go Home After Unrest Over Election Results Leaves Six Dead." *South China Morning Post*, May 22, 2019. www.scmp.com/news/asia/southeast -asia/article/3011281/six-dead-indonesia-riots-election-results-released.

Baran, Stanley J., and Dennis K. Davis. *Mass Communication Theory*, 6th ed. Wadsworth Cengage Learning, 2012.

Barreiro, Victor. "The Other Controversies of Nas Daily's Nuseir Yassin." *Rappler*, August 6, 2021. www.rappler.com/technology/features/other-controversies-nas -daily-nuseir-yassin/.

Baulch, Emma, Adriana Matamoros-Fernandez, and Fiona Suwana. "Memetic Persuasion and WhatsAppification in Indonesia's 2019 Presidential Election." *New Media & Technology* (2022).

Becker, Amanda. "On TikTok, Misogyny and White Supremacy Slip Through 'Enforcement Gap'." *PBS News Hour*, August 24, 2021. www.pbs.org/newshour /nation/on-tiktok-misogyny-and-white-supremacy-slip-through-enforcement-gap.

"Behind Vietnam's Anti-Fake News Decree, a Campaign Against Dissent." Accessed June 20, 2022. www.rappler.com/newsbreak/explainers/behind-vietnam-anti-fake -news-decree-campaign-against-dissent/.

Benkler, Yochai, Robert Faris, and Hal Roberts. *Network Propaganda: Manipulation, Disinformation, and Radicalization in American Politics.* Oxford University Press, 2018.

Berberá, Pablo. "How Social Media Reduces Mass Political Polarization. Evidence from Germany, Spain, and the U.S." *APSA*. 2013.

Bernama. "PAS Parti Ajaran Sesat Bawa Fatwa Songsang – Muhyiddin." *MStar*, April 6, 2022. www.mstar.com.my/lokal/semasa/2013/04/06/pas-parti-ajaran-sesat -bawa-fatwa-songsang-muhyiddin

Bernays, Edward Louis. *Engineering of Consent.* University of Oklahoma Press, 1955.

Bernays, Edward Louis. Propaganda. H. Liveright, 1928.

Bernie, Muhammad, and Irwan Syambudi. "Jokowi yang tak jera gaet Influencer Selama Pandemic Covid-19." *Tirto*, January 18, 2021. tirto.id/jokowi-yang-tak- jera-gaet-influencer-selama-pandemi-covid-19-f9jR

Bessi, Alessandro, and Emilio Ferrara. "Social Bots Distort U.S. 2016 U.S. Presidential Election Online Discussion." *First Monday* no. 21 (2016). DOI:10.5210/ fm.v21i11.7090.

Bjola, Corneliu, and James Pamment. *Countering Online Propaganda and Extremism: The Dark Side of Digital Diplomacy.* Taylor & Francis Group, 2018.

Bollier, Sam. "Voting in the 'World's Social Media Capital'." *Aljazeera*, July 2, 2014. www.aljazeera.com/features/2014/7/2/voting-in-the-worlds-social-media-capital.

Brader, Ted, and George E. Marcus. "Emotion and Political Psychology" (2013).

Bradshaw, Samantha, and Philip Howard. "Troops, Trolls, and Troublemakers: A Global Inventory of Organized Social Media Manipulation." *Working Paper* 12 (2017). University of Oxford.

Bradshaw, Samantha, and Philip N. Howard. "Challenging Truth and Trust: A Global Inventory of Organized Social Media Manipulation." *The Computational Propaganda Project* 1 (2018).

Bradshaw, Samantha, Hannah Bailey, and P. Howard. "Industrialized Disinformation: 2020 Global Inventory of Organized Social Media Manipulation: Computational Propaganda Research Project." 2021. demtech.oii.ox.ac.uk/wp-content/uploads/ sites/127/2021/02/CyberTroop-Report20-Draft9.pdf.

Brennan, Jason. "Propaganda About Propaganda." *Critical Review* 29, no. 1 (2017): 34–48.

Briain, Lonán Ó. "Jealous Corona: Social Media, Musical Propaganda and Public Health in Vietnam." *Perfect Beat* 21, no. 2 (2021): 111–17.

Broch, Nathan. "Japanese Dreams in Borneo: Island to Become Industrial Base." *The Sydney Morning Herald*, January 30, 1943. trove.nla.gov.au/newspaper/article/17835067.

Brodie, Richard. *Virus of the Mind: The New Science of the Meme.* Hay House Inc, 2009.

Buehler, Michael. "Islam and Democracy in Indonesia." *Insight Turkey* 11, no. 4 (2009): 51–63. www.insightturkey.com/articles/islam-and-democracy-in-indonesia.

Burhani, Ahmad Najib. "The Banning of Hizbut Tahrir and the Consolidation of Democracy in Indonesia." *Perspective*, no. 71 (2017). www.iseas.edu.sg/images/pdf/ISEAS_Perspective_2017_71.pdf.

Burke, Adam. "New Political Space, Old Tensions: History, Identity and Violence in Rakhine State, Myanmar." *Contemporary Southeast Asia* (2016): 258–83.

Byman, Daniel. *Al Qaeda, the Islamic State, and the Global Jihadist Movement: What Everyone Needs to Know.* What Everyone Needs To Know (R), 2015.

Cahya, Gemma Holliani. "Debates on Hizbut Tahrir Indonesia Trending Topic on Twitter." *The Jakarta Post*, May 8, 2018. www.thejakartapost.com/news/2018/05/08/debates-on-hizbut-tahrir-indonesia-trending-topic-on-twitter.html

"Call for Action: Managing the Infodemic." *World Health Organization*, December 11, 2020. www.who.int/news/item/11-12-2020-call-for-action-managing-the-infodemic.

Capuno, Joseph J. "Dutertenomics: Populism, Progress, and Prospects." *Asian Economic Policy Review* 15, no. 2 (2020): 262–79.

Castronovo, Russ. *Propaganda 1776: Secrets, Leaks, and Revolutionary Communications in Early America.* Oxford Scholarship Online, 2014.

Celoza, Albert F. *Ferdinand Marcos and the Philippines: The Political Economy of Authoritarianism.* Greenwood Publishing Group, 1997.

Chandra, Grace Nadia. "Indonesia to Double the Size of Current's SE Asia's Digital Economy 2030." *Jakarta Globe*, November 18, 2021. jakartaglobe.id/business/indonesia-to-double-the-size-of-current-se-asias-digital-economy-2030/.

Cheong, Niki. "Disinformation as a Response to the 'Opposition Playground'in MALAYSIA." *From Grassroots Activism to Disinformation: Social Media in Southeast Asia* (2020): 63–85.

Cheong, Niki. "Internet-Led Political Journalism: Challenging Hybrid Regime Resilience in Malaysia." In *The Routledge Companion to Political Journalism*, 121–30. Routledge, 2021.

Chin Yong Liow, Joseph. "Political Islam in Malaysia: Problematising Discourse and Practice in the UMNO-PAS 'Islamisation Race'." *Commonwealth & Comparative Politics* 42, no. 2 (2004): 184–205.

Chin Yong Liow, Joseph. *Piety and Politics: Islamism in Contemporary Malaysia.* OUP USA, 2009.

Choi, Kyung-shick, Lee, Claire Seungeun, and Cadigan, Robert. "Spreading Propaganda in Cyberspace: Comparing Cyber-Resource Usage of Al Qaeda and ISIS." *International Journal of Cybersecurity Intelligence & Cybercrime* 1, no. 1 (2018): 21–39.

Chong, Debra. "Accused of Slander, PAS Chief Hadi Says Will Prove DAP's Communism Links in Court." *The Malay Mail*, November 11, 2022. www.malaymail.com/news/malaysia/2022/11/10/accused-of-slander-pas-chief-hadi-says-will-prove-daps-communism-links-in-court/38735.

CNN Indonesia. "7 alasan buruh tolak Omnibus Law: Pesangon hingga hak cuti." Accessed December 17, 2021. www.cnnindonesia.com/nasional/20201005063845–20–554288/7-alasan-buruh-tolak-omnibus-law-pesangon-hingga-hak-cuti.

Coldewey, Devin. "Graphic Video of Suicide Spreads from Facebook to TikTok to YouTube as Platforms Fail Moderation Test." *Tech Crunch*, September 14, 2020. techcrunch.com/2020/09/13/graphic-video-of-suicide-spreads-from-facebook-to-tiktok-to-youtube-as-platforms-fail-moderation-test/?guccounter=1.

Cole, Ben. "Propaganda: Power and Bias." In *The Syrian Information and Propaganda War*, 1–35. Palgrave Macmillan, Cham, 2022.

"Covid-19 Vaccine Does Not Need to be Halal, Ma'ruf Amin Says." *The Jakarta Post*, October 4, 2020. www.thejakartapost.com/news/2020/10/04/covid-19-vaccine-does-not-need-to-be-halal-maruf-amin-says.html.

Crigler, Ann N. *The Affect Effect: Dynamics of Emotion in Political Thinking and Behavior*. University of Chicago Press, 2007.

CrowdTangle Team. CrowdTangle. Facebook, Menlo Park, California, United States. List ID: 980445069485295.

Curato, Nicole. "Flirting with Authoritarian Fantasies? Rodrigo Duterte and the New Terms of Philippine Populism." *Journal of Contemporary Asia* 47, no. 1 (2017): 142–53.

Cyca, Michelle. "23 Important TikTok Stats Marketers Need to Know in 2022." *Hootsuite*, March 9, 2022. blog.hootsuite.com/tiktok-stats/.

Davidson, Desmond. "Sarawak Groups to Processed with Independence Walk." *The Edge Market*, July 22, 2015. www.theedgemarkets.com/article/sarawak-groups-proceed-independence-walk.

Davis, Angelique M., and Rose Ernst. "Racial Gaslighting." *Politics, Groups, and Identities* 7, no. 4 (2017): 761–74. DOI: 10.1080/21565503.2017.1403934.

Davis, Stephanie. "Media Literacy Training for Southeast Asian Communities." *Google in Asia*, October 28, 2021. blog.google/around-the-globe/google-asia/media-literacy-southeast-asia/.

Deck, Andrew. "Artists Across Asia Dream of Becoming Digital Stickers Millionaires." *Rest of World*, January 11, 2022. restofworld.org/2022/artists-dream-of-becoming-digital-sticker-millionaires/.

Department of Statistics Malaysia. Key Findings Population and Housing Census of Malaysia 2020: Administrative District, May 29, 2022. www.dosm.gov.my/v1/index.php?r=column/cthemeByCat&cat=500&bul_id=WEFGYlprNFpVcUdWcXFFWkY3WHhEQT09&menu_id=L0pheU43NWJwRWVSZklWdzQ4TlhUUT09.

DFR Lab. "#BotSpot: Bots Target Malaysian Elections." *DFR Lab*, April 21, 2018. medium.com/dfrlab/botspot-bots-target-malaysian-elections-785a3c25645b.

Dickson, Ben. "Human Help Wanted: Why AI Is Terrible at Content Moderation." *PC Mag*, July 10, 2019. www.pcmag.com/opinions/human-help-wanted-why-ai-is -terrible-at-content-moderation.

Dickson, EJ. "Why Did Facebook Keep a Man's Livestreamed Suicide Up for Hours?" *Rolling Stone*, September 9, 2020. www.rollingstone.com/culture/culture -news/facebook-tiktok-livestream-suicide-1056959/.

Diep, Uyen. "Fact-checking, Vietnamese Style." *Reporting ASEAN*, February 15, 2021. www.reportingasean.net/fact-checking-vietnamese-style/.

Dipa, Arya. "Filmmaker Dandhy Laksono Names 'Hate Speech' Suspect for Tweeting About Clashes in Papua." *The Jakarta Post*, September 27, 2019. www .thejakartapost.com/news/2019/09/27/filmmaker-dandhy-laksono-named-hate -speech-suspect-for-tweeting-about-clashes-in-papua.html.

Dodge, Raymond. "The Psychology of Propaganda." *Religious Education* 15, no. 5 (1920): 241–52.

Doob, Leonard W., and Edward S. Robinson. "Psychology and Propaganda." *The Annals of the American Academy of Political and Social Science* 179, no. 1 (1935): 88–95.

Ellis-Peterson, Hannah. "Malaysia Opposition Leader Investigated Under Fake News Laws." *The Guardian*, May 3, 2018. www.theguardian.com/world/2018/may/03/ malaysia-opposition-leader-investigated-under-fake-news-laws.

El-Muhammady, Ahmad. "External Conflicts and Malaysia's National Security: The Case of Daesh." *The Journal of Defence and Security* 8, no. 1 (2017): 42–II.

Erez, Edna, Peter R. Ibarra, and William F. McDonald. "Transnational Sex Trafficking: Issues and Prospects." *International Review of Victimology* 11, no. 1 (2004): 1–9.

Evangelista, Rafael, and Bruno Fernanda. "WhatsApp and Political Instability in Brazil: Targeted Messages and Political Radicalisation." *Internet Policy Review* 8, no. 4 (2019). policyreview.info/articles/analysis/whatsapp-and-political-instability -brazil-targeted-messages-and-political.

Evans, Grant. *The Politics of Ritual and Remembrance: Laos Since 1975*. University of Hawaii Press, 1998.

Fahmi, Ismail. "Mampukah isu "RS" bertahan dari gempuran Meikarta?" In *Membaca Indonesia*, edited by Ismail Fahmi, 1–10. DE Press, 2019.

Fellows, Erwin W. "'Propaganda:'History of a Word." *American Speech* 34, no. 3 (1959): 182–89.

Fernandez, Prasana Rosaline, Yang Lai Fong, and Usha Devi Rajaratnam. "Framing the Tanjung Piai By-Election in Multilingual Malaysian Newspapers." In *Discursive Approaches to Politics in Malaysia: Legitimising Governance*, 117–37. Singapore: Springer Nature Singapore, 2023.

Fettling, David. "Why No One Speaks Indonesia's Language." *BBC Travel*, July 5, 2018. www.bbc.com/travel/article/20180703-why-no-one-speaks-indonesias -language

Fink, Christina. "Dangerous Speech, Anti-Muslim Violence, and Facebook in Myanmar." *Journal of International Affairs* 71, no. 1.5 (2018): 43–52.

Finneman, Teri, and Ryan J. Thomas." A Family of Falsehood: Deception, Media Hoaxes, and Fake News." *Newspaper Research Journal* 39, no. 3 (2018): 350–61.

Fletcher, William. "The Background of the Meanings of Propaganda." In *Propaganda! The War for Men's Minds: A Survey of Forces Today Shaping Attitudes and Actions*, edited by Herbert Klein, 88–92. Los Angeles City College Press, 1939.

Foxeus, Niklas. "Buddhist Nationalist Sermons in Myanmar: Anti-Muslim Moral Panic, Conspiracy Theories, and Socio-Cultural Legacies." *Journal of Contemporary Asia* (2022): 1–27.

Gazali, Effendi. "The Suharto Regime and Its Fall Through the Eyes of the Local Media." *Gazette (Leiden, Netherlands)* 64, no. 2 (2002): 121–40.

Get Real. Directed by Yew Guan Tan, Channel News Asia, 2020. *Netflix*. www.netflix.com/watch/81477633.

Gilbert, David. "Russian TikTok Influencers Are Being Paid to Spread Kremlin Propaganda." *Vice News*, March 12, 2022. www.vice.com/en/article/epxken/russian-tiktok-influencers-paid-propaganda?utm_medium=social&utm_source=vice_facebook&fbclid=IwAR36–4PZ-OUR6VSLLGBZaIkbJKyBi3WB_6pZcL7–6jf0vxnrjy-dOd2Gj2Js.

Gilbert, David. "Someone Livestreamed the Boulder Shooting. YouTube Isn't Taking It Down." *VICE News*, March 23, 2021. www.vice.com/en/article/wx8vn9/boulder-shooting-livestream-not-being-pulled-by-youtube.

Goldman, René. "Essential Outsiders: Chinese and Jews in the Modern Transformation of Southeast Asia and Central Europe." (1999): 410–13.

Golovchenko, Yevgeniy, Cody Buntain, Gregory Eady, Megan A. Brown, and Joshua A. Tucker. "Cross-Platform State Propaganda: Russian Trolls on Twitter and YouTube During the 2016 US Presidential Election." *The International Journal of Press/Politics* 25, no. 3 (2020): 357–89.

Gomes de Andrade, Norberto Nuno, Dave Pawson, Dan Muriello, Lizzy Donahue, and Jennifer Guadagno. "Ethics and Artificial Intelligence: Suicide Prevention on Facebook." *Philosophy & Technology* 31, no. 4 (2018): 669–84.

Gomez, James. "Social Media Impact on Malaysia's 13th General Election." *Asia Pacific Media Educator* 24, no. 1 (2014): 95–105.

Gover, Angela R., Shannon B. Harper, and Lynn Langton. "Anti-Asian Hate Crime During the COVID-19 Pandemic: Exploring the Reproduction of Inequality." *American Journal of Criminal Justice* 45, no. 4 (2020): 647–67.

Green, Ollie. "How to Use TikTok on PC." March 26, 2020. www.online-tech-tips.com/cool-websites/how-to-use-tiktok-on-pc/#:~:text=To%20access%20TikTok%20on%20PC,right%20to%20find%20more%20content.

Griffin, Emory A Ledbetter, and Glenn Sparks. *A First Look at Communication Theory*, 10th ed. McGraw-Hill Education, 2019.

Griffin, Emory A, Andrew Ledbetter, and Glenn Grayson Sparks. *A First Look at Communication Theory*, 10th ed. McGraw-Hill Publisher, 2018.

Guan, Lee Hock. "Malay Dominance and Opposition Politics in Malaysia." *Southeast Asian Affairs* (2002): 177–95.

Guest Peter, Fishbein Emily, and Lusan Nunu. "Tiktok Is Repeating Facebook's Mistakes in Myanmar." *Rest of the World*, March 18, 2021. restofworld.org/2021/tiktok-is-repeating-facebooks-mistakes-in-myanmar/.

Guinaudeau, Benjamin, Fabio Vottax, and Kevin Munger. "Fifteen Seconds of Fame: TikTok and the Democratization of Mobile Video on Social Media." *Unpublished paper. Disponible en Internet: osf. io/f7ehq/download [Consulta: 7 de Diciembre de 2020]* (2020).

Guzman, Chad De. "Meta's Facebook Algorithm 'Proactively' Promoted Violence Against the Rohingya, New Amnesty International Report Assesrts." *Time*. September 28, 2022. time.com/6217730/myanmar-meta-rohingya-facebook/.

Haciyakupoglu, Gulizar. "Southeast Asia's Battle Against Disinformation." *The Diplomat*, February 12, 2019. thediplomat.com/2019/02/southeast-asias-battle-aga inst-disinformation/.

Hackett, Conrad. "Which Countries Hold Half of the World's Population?" *Pew Research Center*, July 11, 2018. www.pewresearch.org/fact- tank/2014/07/11/half -the-worlds-population-live-in-just-6-countries/.

Halidi, Risna. "Mengenal Empat Pilar Literasi Digital Serta Pengertiannya." *Suara*. September 02, 2021. www.suara.com/lifestyle/2021/09/02/232441/mengenal -empat-pilar-literasi-digital-serta-pengertiannya.

Halim, Devina. "Admin Akun Instagram "Suara Rakyat" Mengaku Buat 843 Meme Hoaks." *Kompas*. November 23, 2018. nasional.kompas.com/read/2018/11/23 /23560191/admin-akun-instagram-suara-rakyat-mengaku-buat-843-meme-hoaks ?page=all.

Hamid, Abdul. "Jokowi's Populism in 2012 Gubernatorial Election." *Journal of Current Southeast Asian Affairs* 33, no. 1 (2014): 85–109. DOI: 10.1177%2F18681034 1403300106.

Hanan, Djayadi. "Making Presidentialism Work: Legislative and Executive Inter-action in Indonesian Democracy." Electronic Thesis or Dissertation, 2012. etd .ohiolink.edu/.

Haqqi, Achmad. "Propaganda Firehose of Falsehood Pada Pemilu 2019 di Indone-sia." *WACANA: Jurnal Ilmiah Ilmu Komunikasi* 19, no. 2 (2020): 175–85.

Hasbullah. "Mendikbud larang penggunaan hijab di sekolah." *Times Indonesia*, February 21, 2021. www.timesindonesia.co.id/read/news/329386/cek-fakta -mendikbud-larang-penggunaan-hijab-di-sekolah.

Hasono, Norman. "Despite Improvements, Indonesia's Digital Literacy Remains Low." *The Jakarta Post*, January 20, 2022. www.thejakartapost.com/business/2022 /01/20/despite-improvements-indonesias-digital-literacy-remains-low.html#:~:text =Digital%20literacy%20in%20Indonesia%20has,by%20the%20COVID%2D19 %20pandemic.

Hassan, Tamer. "Here's How to Identify a Bot." *Techradar*, October 03, 2020. www .techradar.com/news/heres-how-to-spot-a-bot.

Heder, Steve, and Judy Ledgerwood. *Propaganda, Politics and Violence in Cambodia: Democratic Transition Under United Nations Peace-Keeping: Democratic Transition Under United Nations Peace-Keeping*. Routledge, 2016.

Heller, Rafael. "Understanding Propaganda: A Conversation with Renee Hobbs." *Phi Delta Kappan* 102, no. 5 (2021): 33–37.

Herdiansah, Ari Ganjar, Luthfi Hamzah Husin, and Hendra. "Religious Identity Politics on Social Media in Indo-nesia: A Discursive Analysis on Islamic Civil

Societies." *Jurnal Studi Pemerintahan* 9, no. 2 (2018): 187–222. journal.umy.ac.id
/index.php/jsp/article/view/3934.

Heriyanto, Devina. "The Rise of 'kadrun' and 'togog': Why Political Polarization
in Indonesian Is Far from Over." *The Jakarta Post*. November 20, 2019. www
.thejakartapost.com/news/2019/11/19/the-rise-of-kadrun-and-togog-why-political
-polarization-in-indonesia-is-far-from-over.html.

Heryanto, Ariel. "The Debris of Post-Authoritarianism in Indonesia." In *Democracy
and Civil Society in Asia: Volume 2*, 65–85. London: Palgrave Macmillan, 2004.

Hidayat, Ferry. "Trimedya di-WA Ganjar, 'saya kasih sticker bergambar mbak Puan
lagi angkat jempol', lalu dia balas." *Warta Ekonomi*, June 6, 2022. wartaekono
mi.co.id/read419040/trimedya-di-wa-ganjar-saya-kasih-sticker-bergambar-mbak
-puan-lagi-angkat-jempol-lalu-dia-balas.

Hogan, Libby, and Michael Safi. "Revealed: Facebook Hate Speech Exploded
in Myanmar During Rohingya Crisis." *The Guardian*, April 3, 2018. www
.theguardian.com/world/2018/apr/03/revealed-facebook-hate-speech-exploded-in
-myanmar-during-rohingya-crisis.

Hopkins, Julian. "Cybertroopers and Tea Parties: Government Use of the Internet in
Malaysia." *Asian Journal of Communication* 24, no. 1 (2014): 5–24.

Howard, Philip N., Samuel Woolley, and Ryan Calo. "Algorithms, Bots, and Political
Communication in the US 2016 Election: The Challenge of Automated Political
Communication for Election Law and Administration." *Journal of Information
Technology & Politics* 15, no. 2 (2018): 81–93.

HRW. "Indonesia: New Criminal Code Disastrous for Rights." *Human Rights Watch*.
December 8, 2022. www.hrw.org/news/2022/12/08/indonesia-new-criminal-code
-disastrous-rights.

Hunt, Sarah. "Bufallo's Protest Hurts Indonesian President's Feelings." *Reuters*.
February 5, 2010. www.reuters.com/article/us-indonesia-buffalo-idUSTRE6132
TB20100204.

Hutt, David. "Are Southeast Asia's Anti-China Nationalists Democrats?" *The
Diplomat*, November 3, 2020. thediplomat.com/2020/11/are-southeast-asias-anti-c
hina-nationalists-democrats/.

Idris, Ika Karlina. "Ada hoaks di balik demo: membedah keberhasilan strategi
gaslighting pemerintah." *The Conversation*, October 28, 2020. theconversation
.com/ada-hoaks-di-balik-demo-membedah-keberhasilan-strategi-gaslighting-pem
erintah-148533.

Idris, Ika Karlina. "Indonesia's Misinformation Program Undermines More than It
Teaches." *360info*. February 14, 2022. 360info.org/indonesias-misinformation-pr
ogram-undermines-more-than-it-teaches/.

Idris, Ika karlina. "Mengenali jaringan penyebar hoax." *Kompas*, February 26, 2019.

Idris, Ika Karlina. "Narasi pandemi di ruang publik baru Asia Tenggara: Di antara
kisah kepahlawanana dan narasi anti-china." In *Demokrasi dan Pandemi: Bunga
Rampai Pengetahuan Masyarakat Sipil di Indonesia*. Perhimpunan Pengembangan
Media Nusantara, 2021.

Idris, Ika Karlina. The Illusion of a Public Sphere: The Indonesian Government
Communication on Social Media. Dissertation, 2019. etd.ohiolink.edu/.

Idris, Ika Karlina, and Abdul Malik Gismar. "TikTok: ruang baru ekspresi dan negosiasi identitas local Gen Z Indonesia." *The Conversation*, August 24, 2021. theconversation.com/tiktok-ruang-baru-ekspresi-dan-negosiasi-identitas-lokal-gen -z-indonesia-165883.

Idris, Ika Karlina, and Muhamad Risqi Saputra. "How Indonesians Politicians Misuse 'Big Data' to Delay the Next Presidential Election." *The Jakarta Post*, March 23, 2022. www.thejakartapost.com/opinion/2022/03/23/how-indonesian-politicians -misuse-big-data-to-delay-the-next-presidential-election.html.

Idris, Ika Karlina, and Nuurrianti Jalli. "How Blaming Others Dominates Indonesian and Malaysian Twitterspheres During COVID-19 Pandemic." *The Conversation*, April 28, 2020. theconversation.com/how-blaming-others-dominates-indonesian- and-malaysian-twitterspheres-during-covid-19-pandemic-136193.

Idris, Ika Karlina, Nuurrianti Jalli, and Sabariah Mohammad Salleh. "Blaming Others: Stigmas Related to COVID-19 Pandemic in Indonesia and Malaysia." *Malaysian Journal of Communication* 38, no. 4 (2022): 338–54.

"Imbangi hoax dan hate speech, satgas medsos K/L RI siap publikasikan konten positif." *BKN*, May 24, 2018. www.bkn.go.id/berita/imbangi-hoax-dan-hate -speech-satgas-medsos-kl-ri-siap-publikasikan-konten-positif.

"Indonesian Forest Fires Crisis: Palm Oil and Pulp Companies with Largest Burned Land Areas Are Going Unpunished." *Greenpeace*, September 24, 2019. www .greenpeace.org/southeastasia/publication/3106/3106/.

"Indonesia pengguna WhatsApp terbesar ketiga di dunia." *Katadata*, October 27, 2021. databoks.katadata.co.id/datapublish/2021/11/23/indonesia-pengguna-what sapp-terbesar-ketiga-di-dunia.

"Indonesia: Thousands Protest Against 'Omnibus Law' on Jobs." *BBC Indonesia, BBC*, October 8, 2020. www.bbc.com/news/world-asia-54460090.

Indonesian Hoaxes, August 26, 2018. www.facebook.com/705618876157312/posts /2008873479165172.

Indonesian Hoaxes, September 18, 2018. www.facebook.com/705618876157312/ posts/2038646499521203.

Indonesian Hoaxes. September 20, 2018. www.facebook.com/705618876157312/ posts/1604763986242792.

Irawanto, Budi. "Making It Personal: The Campaign Battle on Social Media in Indonesia's 2019 Presidential Election." *ISEAS Yusof Ishak Institute* 28 (2019): 1–11.

ISEAS Yusof-Ishak. "Webinar on "Creating Chaos and Consent: Cyber Troops and Organised Propaganda in Indonesia's Cybersphere." ISEAS Yusof Ishak Institute, September 21, 2021. www.iseas.edu.sg/media/event-highlights/webinar -on-creating-chaos-and-consent-cyber-troops-and-organised-propaganda-in -indonesias-cybersphere/

Iwaichi, Fujiwara. *Kikan F: Japanese Army Intelligence Operations in Southeast Asia During World War. II*, 1983.

Jalli, Nuurrianti, and Ika Karlina Idris. "Fake News and Elections in Two Southeast Asian Nations: A Comparative Study of Malaysia General Election 2018 and Indonesia Presidential Election 2019." In *International Conference on Democratisation in Southeast Asia (ICDeSA 2019)*, 138–48. Atlantis Press, 2019.

Jalli, Nuurrianti, Siti Aeisha Joharry, and Sabariah Mohamed Salleh. "ICERD in Malaysian Online News Reports: Analysis of Rhetoric and Public Opinion." *Social Sciences & Humanities Open* 6, no. 1 (2022): 100318.

Jalli, Nuurrianti, Triana Leong, Meeko Angela Camba, and Yik Wai Chee. "TikTok Consumption of Information Among Gen-Z in Malaysia, Indonesia, and the Philippines." *Tech Camp*, 2021. sites.google.com/view/techcamp-tiktok/home.

Jalli, Nuurrianti. "The Effectiveness of Social Media in Assisting Opinion Leaders to Disseminate Political Ideologies in Developing Countries: The Case of Malaysia." *Jurnal Komunikasi: Malaysian Journal of Communication* 32, no. 1 (2016): 551–79.

Jalli, Nuurrianti. 'TikTok Is Propagandists' New Tool to Win Elections in Southeast Asia." *The Conversation*, March 25, 2022. theconversation.com/tiktok-is-propa gandists-new-tool-to-win-elections-in-southeast-asia-179684.

Jalli, Nuurrianti. "Disinformation and Democracy in Malaysia." In *Democracy in Asia*, edited by Ryan Hass, and Patricia Kim, 44–42. Washington, DC: Brookings Institution, 2022. www.brookings.edu/product/democracy-in-asia/.

Jalli, Nuurrianti. "How TikTok Became a Breeding Ground for Hate Speech in the Latest Malaysia General Election." *The Conversation*, March 23, 2023. theconvers ation.com/how-tiktok-became-a-breeding-ground-for-hate-speech-in-the-latest -malaysia-general-election-200542.

Jalli, Nuurrianti. "Three Fact-Checking Challenges in Southeast Asia." *The Conversation*, October 26, 2020. theconversation.com/three-fact-checking-chall enges-in-southeast-asia-148738.

Jalli, Nuurrianti. "Three Fact-Checking Challenges in Southeast Asia." *The Conversation*, October 27, 2020. theconversation.com/three-fact-checking-chall enges-in-southeast-asia-148738.

Jalli, Nuurrianti. "Tiktok Is Propagandists' New Tool to Win Elections in Southeast Asia." *The Conversation*, April 1, 2022. theconversation.com/profiles/nuurrianti-jalli-734757/articles.

Jalli, Nuurrianti. *Media and Politics: Students' Attitudes and Experts' Opinions Towards Citizen Journalism and Political Outcomes in Malaysia*. Ohio University, 2017.

Jayakumar, Shashi, Benjamin Ang, and Nur Diyanah Anwar. "Fake News and Disinformation: Singapore Perspectives." In *Disinformation and Fake News*, 137–58. Singapore: Palgrave Macmillan, 2021.

Jeffriando, Maikel, and Wilda Asmarini. "Indonesian Protesters Disperse After Second Night of Post-election Unrest." *Reuters*, May 23, 2019. www.reuters.com/article/us-indonesia-election-idUSKCN1ST003.

Jerit, Jennifer. "Survival of the Fittest: Rhetoric During the Course of an Election Campaign." *Political psychology* 25, no. 4 (2004): 563–75.

Johns, Amelia, and Niki Cheong. "The Affective Pressure of WhatsApp: From Safe Spaces to Conspirational Publics. *Journal of Media & Cultural Studies* 35, no. 5 (2021): 732–46. DOI: 10.1080/10304312.2021.1983256.

Jones, David Seth. "ASEAN and Transboundary Haze Pollution in Southeast Asia." *Asia Europe Journal* 4, no. 3 (2006): 431–46.

Joo-Jock, Lim. "Brunei: Prospects for a" Protectorate." *Southeast Asian Affairs* (1976): 149–64.

Jowett, Garth, and Victoria O'Donnel. *Propaganda and Persuasion*, 3rd.ed. Sage Publications, 1999.

Jowett, Garth S., and Victoria O'Donnell. *Propaganda and Persuasion*. Sage Publications, 2018.

Jung, Eun Ji, and Seongcheol Kim. "Suicide on YouTube: Factors Engaging Viewers to a Selection of Suicide-Themed Videos." *PLOS One* 16, no. 6 (2021): e0252796.

Kalsnes, Bente. "The Social Media Paradox Explained: Comparing Political Parties' Facebook Strategy Versus Practice." *Social Media+ Society* 2, no. 2 (2016).

"Kasus Saracen: Pesan kebencian dan hoax di media sosial memang terorganisir." *BBC Indonesia*, August 23, 2017. www.bbc.com/indonesia/trensosial-41022914.

Kepel, Gilles. *Jihad: The Trail of Political Islam*. Harvard University Press, 2002.

"KFC didakwa tidak halal." *Sebenarnya*, January, 2017. sebenarnya.my/kfc-didakwa -tidak-halal/.

Khan, M. Laeeq, and Ika Karlina Idris. "Recognise Misinformation and Verify Before Sharing: A Reasoned Action and Information Literacy Perspective." *Behaviour & Information Technology* 38, no. 12 (2019): 1194–1212. DOI: 10.1080/0144929X.2019.1578828.

Kho, Kathleen Rose Gatchalian. "Behavioural Biases and Identity in Social Media: The Case of Philippine Populism, President Duterte's Rise, and Ways Forward." (2019).

Khoo, Boo Teik. "Borne by Dissent, Tormented by Divides: The Opposition 60 Years after Merdeka." *Southeast Asian Studies* 7, no. 3 (2018): 471–91.

Kollanyi, Bence, Philip N. Howard, and Samuel C. Woolley. "Bots and Automation Over Twitter During the First US Presidential Debate." *Comprop data memo* 1 (2016): 1–4.

"Kominfo ajak anak muda perkuat literasi digital masyarakat." *Kominfo*, December 15, 2021. www.kominfo.go.id/content/detail/38766/kominfo-ajak-anak-muda -perkuat-literasi-digital-masyarakat/0/berita_satker

Kovach, Bill, and Tom Rosenstiel. *Elements of Journalism: What News People Should Know and the Public Should Expect*. Random House, 2014.

"Kunjungi Kemensetneg dan KSP, Kolaborasi #IndonesiaBicaraBaik dengan Perhumas." *Perhumas*, September 2, 2019. www.perhumas.or.id/kunjungan -perhumas-ke-kemensetneg-dan-ksp/.

Kurnia, Tommy. "Rudiantara tak tahu Kominfo dukung kampanye sawit baik." *Liputan6com*, September 17, 2019. www.liputan6.com/bisnis/read/4064590/ rudiantara-tak-tahu-kominfo-dukung-kampanye-sawit-baik.

Lam, Lydia. "Singapore Under Highest Terror Threat in Recent Years: 8 Key Points from MHA's Terror Report." *The Straits Times* (2017).

Lamb, Kate, and Ananda Teresia. "Explainer: Why Is Indonesia's New Criminal Code So Controversial?" *Reuters*, December 6, 2022. www.reuters.com/world/ asia-pacific/why-is-indonesias-new-criminal-code-so-controversial-2022–12–06/.

Lamb, Kate. "Muslim Cyber Army: A 'Fake News' Operation Designed to Derail Indonesia's Leader." *The Guardian*, March 13, 2018. www.theguardian.com/world

/2018/mar/13/muslim-cyber-army-a-fake-news-operation-designed-to-bring-down -indonesias-leader.

Lamprianou, Iasonas, and Antonis A. Ellinas. "Emotion, Sophistication and Political Behavior: Evidence from a Laboratory Experiment." *Political Psychology* 40, no. 4 (2019): 859–76.

Lasswell, Harold D. "The Theory of Political Propaganda." *American Political Science Review* 21, no. 3 (1927): 627–31.

Lasswell, Harold D. *Propaganda Technique in the World War*. Garland Publishing, 1972.

Lasswell, Harold D. *World Politics and Personal Insecurity*. University of Chicago Press, 1934.

Latiff, Rozana, and Mei Mei Chu. "TikTok on 'High Alert' in Malaysia as Tensions Rise Over Election Wrangle." *Reuters*. November 23, 2022. www.reuters.com/ world/asia-pacific/tiktok-high-alert-malaysia-tensions-rise-over-election-wrangle -2022-11-23/.

"LBH Pers condemns minister for calling jobs law criticism hoaxes." *The Jakarta Post*, October 16, 2020. www.thejakartapost.com/news/2020/10/16/lbh-pers -condemns-minister-for-calling-jobs-law-criticisms-hoaxes.html.

Lee Roth, Andy, and Liam O'Connell. "Omission Is the Same as Permission." *Index on Censorship* 50, no. 4 (2021): 24–27.

Lee, Poh Ping. "Malaysia in 2015: A Denouement of Sorts for the Prime Minister." *Asian Survey* 56, no. 1 (2016): 101–107.

Lema, Karen, and Enrico Dela Cruz. "Philippines Election Winner Marcos Tells World to Judge Him by Actions, Not Family's Past." *Reuters*, May 11, 2022. www .reuters.com/world/asia-pacific/philippines-election-win-returns-marcos-power -polarisation-2022-05-10/.

"Lemhanas turut aktif dalam tim SIMAN." *Lemhanas RI*, September 8, 2018. www.lemhannas.go.id/index.php/berita/item/525-lemhannas-turut-aktif-dalam-tim -siman-sinergi-media-sosial-aparatur-negara.html

Leong, Pauline Pooi Yin. "Digital Mediatization and the Sharpening of Malaysian Political Contests." In *Digital Mediatization and the Sharpening of Malaysian Political Contests*. ISEAS Publishing, 2021.

Leong, Pauline Pooi Yin. "New Media and Political Change." In *Malaysian Politics in the New Media Age*, 147–60. Singapore: Springer, 2019.

Lim, How Pim. "Sarawak's population Rises to Over 2.56 Million in 2020." *The Borneo Post*, June 16, 2022. www.theborneopost.com/2022/06/16/sarawaks -population-rises-to-over-2-56-mln-in-2020/.

Ling, Sharon. "NGO: Restore Sarawak Rights or Risk a Secession Movement." *The Star*, July 22, 2019. www.thestar.com.my/news/nation/2019/07/22/ngo-restore -sarawak-rights-or-risk-a-secession-movement.

"Literasi digital netizen fair dan siberkreasi award 2021: Puncak rangkaian literasi digital nasional." *Kominfo*, December 20, 2021. kominfo.go.id/content/detail /38869/siaran-pers-no-458hmkominfo122021-tentang-literasi-digital-netizen-fair -dan-sibekreasi-award-2021-puncak-rangkaian-literasi-digital-nasional/0/siaran_ pers.

Little, Andrew T. "Fake News, Propaganda, and Lies Can Be Pervasive Even If They Aren't Persuasive." *Critique* 11, no. 1 (2018): 21–34.

Lowe, Aya. "How Mafindo Went From a Grassroots Movement to a National Fact-Checking Outlet." *Meta News Partnership APAC*, June 12, 2019. www.facebook .com/journalismproject/mafindo-facebook-third-party-fact-checking.

Lukito, Josephine, Zhe Cui, An Hu, Taeyoung Lee, and Joao VS Ozawa. "States vs. Social Movements: Protests and State Repression in Asia." *Media and Communication* 10, no. 4 (2022): 5–17.

"Mahasiswa UNHI diajak melek literasi keuangan digital, cegah jadi korban pinjol." *Kumparan*, October 23, 2021. kumparan.com/kumparannews/mahasiswa-unhi-diaj ak-melek-literasi-keuangan-digital-cegah-jadi-korban-pinjol-1wmDf9x0bbs/2.

Malik, Maszlee. *'Kafir Harbi'in Malaysia: Another Path to Polarization.* ISEAS-Yusof Ishak Institute, 2017 (4).

Maulana, Azis, and Catur Nugroho. "Nasionalisme Dalam Narasi Cerita Film (Analisis Narasi Tzvetan Todorov Pada Film Habibie and Ainun)." *ProTVF* 2, no. 1 (2018): 37–49.

Mauzy, Diane K. "The 1982 General Elections in Malaysia: A Mandate for Change?" *Asian Survey* 23, no. 4 (1983): 497–517.

Maweu, Jacinta Maweu. "Fake Elections'? Cyber Propaganda, Disinformation and the 2017 General Elections in Kenya." *African Journalism Studies* 40, no. 4 (2020): 62–76.

"May 13, Never Again." *Malaysia Kini*. May 13, 2019. pages.malaysiakini.com/may13/en/.

McCombs, Maxwell E., and Donald L. Shaw. "The Agenda-Setting Function of Mass Media." *Public Opinion Quarterly* 36, no. 2 (1972): 176–87.

McDaniel, Drew. O. *Electronic Tigers of Southeast Asia: The Politics of Media, Technology, and National Development.* Iowa: Iowa State University Press, 2004.

McKirdy, Euan. "Philippines Terror Group Abu Sayyaf Releases 'Final' Hostage Video." *CNN*, May 24, 2016. edition.cnn.com/2016/05/23/asia/abu-sayyaf-final-h ostage-video/index.html.

Medistiara, Yulida. "TKN: Jokowi Bongkar Strategi Firehose of Falsehood, Rakyat Jangan Tertipu." February 4, 2021. news.detik.com/berita/d-4413064/tkn-jokowi -bongkar-strategi-firehose-of-falsehood-rakyat-jangan-tertipu.

"Mengulik data suku di Indonesia." *BPS*, 2015. www.bps.go.id/news/2015/11/18/127 /mengulik-data-suku-di-indonesia.html.

"Menteri Johnny: Orkestrasi komunikasi publik dukung penanganan pandemi." Kominfo. August 10, 2021. kominfo.go.id/content/detail/36277/siaran-pers -no-274hmkominfo082021-tentang-menteri-johnny-orkestrasi-komunikasi-p ublik-dukung-penanganan-pandemi/0/siaran_persMichella, Widya. "MUI akan sertifikasi seluruh DAI di Indonesia." Sindonews. April 27, 2021. nasional.sindon ews.com/read/410674/15/mui-akan-sertifikasi-seluruh-dai-di-indonesia-161952 5056.

Meta. "Taking Down Coordinated Inauthentic Behaviour in Indonesia." *Meta*, January 31, 2019. about.fb.com/news/2019/01/taking-down-coordinated-inaut hentic-behavior-in-indonesia/.

Milmo, Dan. "Rohingya sue Facebook for £150bn Over Myanmar Genocide." *The Guardian*, December 6, 2021. www.theguardian.com/technology/2021/dec/06/rohingya-sue-facebook-myanmar-genocide-us-uk-legal-action-social-media-violence.

Minh, Nhat. "Vietnam Has Anti-Fake News Center." *Hanoi Times*, January 31, 2021. hanoitimes.vn/vietnam-has-anti-fake-news-center-315877.html.

Mohd Sani, Mohd Azizuddin, and Knocks Tapiwa Zengeni. "Democratisation in Malaysia: The Impact of Social Media in the 2008 General Election." (2010): 1–16.

Mohsen, Amar Shah. "Netizens Raise Alarm Over May 13 Hate Content Posted on TikTok." *The Vibes.Com. The Vibes*, November 23, 2022. www.thevibes.com/articles/news/78211/netizens-raise-alarm-over-may-13-hate-content-posted-on-tiktok.

Moidin, Shofiyyah, Nur Auni Syafiqah Ismail, Muhammad Syukri Mohd Ashmir Wong, Nur Hafizah Harun, and Norazlina Mamat. "A Study on Factors of Fake News Spreading on the Halal Status of Food Products in Malaysia." *Jurnal 'Ulwan* 6, no. 3, 2021.

Moir, Nathaniel L. "ISIL Radicalization, Recruitment, and Social Media Operations in Indonesia, Malaysia, and the Philippines." *PRISM* 7, no. 1 (2017): 90–107.

Moloney, Kevin. *Rethinking Public Relations: PR, Propaganda, and Democracy.* New York: Routledge, 2006.

Money-Kyrle, Roger. "The Psychology of Propaganda." *British Journal of Medical Psychology* 19, no. 1 (1941): 82–94.

Mulyanto, Randy. "Why Are Indonesian Protesting the Omnibus Law If Jokowi Says It Will Boost Jobs and Investments?" *South China Morning Press*, August 20, 2020. www.scmp.com/week-asia/explained/article/3098094/indonesia-says-omnibus-law-will-create-jobs-attract-foreign.

Munggaran, Abdi. "Industri Sawit di Mata Netizen." In *Membaca Indonesia*, edited by Ismail Fahmi, 1–10. DE Press, 2019.

Muninggar, Sri Saraswati. "The Political Campaign Industry and the Rise of Disinformation in Indonesia." In *Grassroot Activism to Disinformation in Southeast Asia*, edited by Aim Sinpeng, and Ross Tapsell. ISEAS-Yusof Ishaq Institute, 2020.

Mustapa Kamal, Shazwan. "How Racial Misinformation Shapes Politics, According to an ex-BN 'cybertrooper'." *Malay Mail*, October 05, 2018. www.malaymail.com/news/malaysia/2018/10/05/how-racial-misinformation-shapes-politics-according-to-an-ex-bn-cybertroope/1679778.

Myint, Moe. "A Year Later, Myanmar's Fact-Checkers Try to Catch Up with COVID-19 Infodemic." *Reporting ASEAN*, December 24, 2021. www.reportingasean.net/a-year-later-fact-checkers-try-to-catch-up-with-covid-19-infodemic/.

Nassar, Tamara, and Ali Abunimah. "How Nas Daily whitewashes Israel's Crimes." *The Electronic Intifada*, December 21, 2020. electronicintifada.net/content/how-nas-daily-whitewashes-israels-crimes/31936.

"Najib blames Dr M and Muhyiddin Govts for Debt Hitting RM1trillion." *The Star.* Accessed August 22, 2022. www.thestar.com.my/news/nation/2022/03/03/najib-blames-dr-m-and-muhyiddin-govts-for-debt-hitting-rm1trillion.

Neo, Ric. "A Cudgel of Repression: Analysing State Instrumentalization of the 'Fake News' Label in Southeast Asia." *Journalism*. DOI: 10.1177/1464884920984060.

Neyazi, Taberez Ahmed. "Digital Propaganda, Political Bots and Polarized Politics in India, Asian." *Journal of Communication* 30, no. 1 (2020): 39–57. DOI: 10.1080/01292986.2019.1699938.

Nguitragool, Paruedee. "Negotiating the Haze Treaty: Rationality and Institutions in the Negotiations for the ASEAN Agreement on Transboundary Haze Pollution (2002)." *Asian Survey* 51, no. 2 (2011): 356–78.

Niewenhuis, Lucas. "The Difference Between TikTok and Douyin." *Sup China*, September 15, 2019. supchina.com/2019/09/25/the-difference-between-tiktok-and-douyin/.

Nilsen, Marte, and Shintaro Hara. "Religious Motivation in Political Struggles." *Journal of Religion and Violence* 5, no. 3 (2017): 291–311.

Nizam, Fuad. "Police Report Lodged Against Hadi for His 'DAP Is Pro-Communist' Remarks." *New Straits Times*, November 9, 2022. www.nst.com.my/news/politics/2022/11/849038/police-report-lodged-against-hadi-his-dap-pro-communist-remarks.

Normala, Adinda. "Indonesia Considers Stopping Palm Oil Exports to the E.U." *Jakarta Globe*, May 26, 2018. jakartaglobe.id/context/indonesia-considers-stopping-palm-oil-exports-to-the-european-union/.

Notley, Tanya. "Misinformation Won't Go Away, But Media Literacy Can Help It." *360info*, February 14, 2022. 360info.org/misinformation-wont-go-away-but-media-literacy-can-help-fight-it/.

Nugraheny, Dian Erika. "56 pegawai KPK dipecat, Jokowi: Jangan apa-apa ditarik ke Presiden." *Kompas*, September 16, 2021. nasional.kompas.com/read/2021/09/16/11591351/56-pegawai-kpk-dipecat-jokowi-jangan-apa-apa-ditarik-ke-presiden?page=all.

Nurfaizah, Siti. "Misbakhun Berbagi Jurus Kampanye Positif Sawit Via Medsos." *Akurat*, September 17, 2019. akurat.co/misbakhun-berbagi-jurus-kampanye-positif-sawit-via-medsos.

O'Neil, Matt. "Presidential Candidates Go Viral in Indonesia's Social Media Election." *ABC*, July 2, 2014. www.abc.net.au/radionational/programs/saturdayextra/indonesia's-social-media-elections/5566416.

Ojebode, A., and W. Oladapo. "The Power of Truth-Drive Propaganda: A Rhetorical Criticism of Governor Ajimobi's Political Slogan:" ki oyo le da'a ajumose gbogbo wa ni."" (2014).

Olivier, Bob. "The Factors Driving Islamisation in Malaysia." *Islamic Revivalism and Politics in Malaysia: Problems in Nation Building* (2020): 59–92.

Ong, Jonathan Corpus, and Samuel Cabbuag. "Pseudonymous Influencers and Horny'Alts' in the Philippines: Media Manipulation Beyond Fake News." *The Journal of Socio-Technical Critique* 2, no. 2 (2022).

Onn, Lee Poh, and Kevin Zhang. "2021/165 "What Awaits Sarawak in the State Election?" by Lee Poh Onn and Kevin Zhang" ISEAS Yusof Ishak Institute, 2021. www.iseas.edu.sg/articles-commentaries/iseas-perspective/2021–165-what-awaits-sarawak-in-the-state-election-by-lee-poh-onn-and-kevin-zhang/.

"Orkestrasi agenda komunikasi publik untuk presidensi G20, pranata humas menjadi punggawa." *Iprahumas*, January 30, 2022. www.iprahumas.id/detailpost /orkestrasi-agenda-komunikasi-publik-untuk-presidensi-g20-pranata-humas -menjadi-punggawa.

Osman, Mohamed Nawab Mohamed, and Prashant Waikar. "Fear and Loathing: Uncivil Islamism and Indonesia's Anti-Ahok Movement." *Indonesia* 106 (2018): 89–109.

Papacharissi, Z. *A Private Sphere: Democracy in a Digital Age*. Polity Press, 2010.

Paul, Christopher, and Matthews Miriam. "Defending Against Russian Propaganda." *The SAGE Handbook of Propaganda* (2019): 286.

Paul, Christopher, and Miriam Matthews. "The Russian "Firehose of Falsehood" Propaganda Model." *Rand Corporation* 2, no. 7 (2016): 1–10.

"Pemerintah tingkatkan peran sinergi media sosial untuk aparatur negara." *Kominfo*, January 15, 2019. www.kominfo.go.id/content/detail/15928/pemerintah-tingkatkan -peran-sinergi-media-sosial-untuk-aparatur-negara/0/berita.

"Penguatan peran pranat humas Indonesia." *YouTube Unpad*, December 17, 2022. www.youtube.com/watch?v=1NKnACzdVfQ&t=2858s.

"Perhumas genjot sertifikasi dan akreditas." *Perhumas*, August 2, 2017. www .perhumas.or.id/profesi-public-relations-perhumas-genjot-sertifikasi-dan -akreditasi/.

"Perhumas kukuhkan badan pengurus pusat 2017–2020." *Perhumas*, March 7, 2018. www.perhumas.or.id/perhumas-kukuhkan-badan-pengurus-pusat-2017–2020/.

Peter Lentini. "Antipodal Terrorists?" *In The Globalization of Political Violence: Globalization's Shadow*, edited by Richard Devetak, and Christopher Wo Hughes, 197–218. London: Routledge, 2008.

Pierson, David. "Dictator's Son Uses TikTok to Lead in Philippine Election and Rewrite His Family's Past." *Los Angeles Times*, May 5, 2022. www .latimes.com/world-nation/story/2022–05–05/dictators-son-uses-tiktok-to-lead- philippines-election-and-rewrite-his-familys-past.

"Polisi tangkap penyebar hoaks demo pekerja China di Morowali." *CNN Indonesia*, January 30, 2019. www.cnnindonesia.com/nasional/20190130145327–12–365076/ polisi-tangkap-penyebar-hoaks-demo-pekerja-china-di-morowali.

Postman, Neil. Technopoly: The surrender of culture to technology. Vintage, 2011.

Potkins, Fanny. "'I Will Shoot Whoever I See': Myanmar Soldiers Use TikTok to Threaten Protesters." *Reuters*, March 4, 2021. www.reuters.com/article/ us-myanmar-tiktok/i-will-shoot-whoever-i-see-myanmar-soldiers-use-tiktok-to -threaten-protesters-idUSKBN2AW17X.

Potkins, Fanny. "TikTok Booms in Southeast Asia As It Picks Path Through Political Minefields." *Reuters*, August 28, 2020. www.reuters.com/article/us-tiktok -southeastasia-idUSKBN25O033.

Prabowo, Dani. "Prabowo dan Jokowi antithesis SBY." *Kompas*, June 11, 2014. nasional.kompas.com/read/2014/06/11/1516341/Prabowo.dan.Jokowi.Antitesis .SBY.

Prakash, G. "Report: Malaysian Cybertrooper Teams Employ Full-Time Staff, Used by Politicians and Businesses Alike." *Malay Mail*, January 14, 2021. www

.malaymail.com/news/malaysia/2021/01/14/report-malaysian-cybertrooper-teams
-employ-full-time-staff-used-by-politici/1940305.

"Prihatin maraknya kabar bohong, Presiden setuju Gerakan Indonesia bicara baik." *Kominfo*, December 10, 2018. www.kominfo.go.id/content/detail/15592/ prihatin-maraknya-kabar-bohong-presiden-setuju-gerakan-indonesia-bicara-baik /0/berita.

Priyatna, Centurion Chandratama, Fajar Syuderajat, and Aang Koswara. "Evaluasi tenaga humas pemerintah oleh Kementerian Komunikasi dan Informatika." *PRofesi Humas* 5, no. 1 (2020): 58–81. jurnal.unpad.ac.id/profesi-humas/article/view/23745.

Puddington, Arch, and Tyler Roylance. "Freedom in the World 2017." *Freedom House.* 2017. freedomhouse.org/sites/default/files/FH_FIW_2017_Report_Final.pdf.

Purba, David Oliver. "Pernyataan lengkap Ratna Sarumpat yang mengakui berbohong dianiaya." *Kompas*, October 3, 2018. megapolitan.kompas.com/read/2018/10/03/1 7395561/pernyataan-lengkap-ratna-sarumpaet-yang-mengaku-berbohong-dianiaya

Purnamasari, Niken. "Grace Natalie tentang 'Hulk' Rilis Video Panasnya dengan Ahok." *Detik*, June 8, 2018. news.detik.com/berita/d-4059710/grace-natalie-tant ang-hulk-rilis-video-panasnya-dengan-ahok.

Putra, Nanda Perdana. "Polisi Tangkap Admin Instagram SR23 Penyebar Jokowi PKI." *Liputan*, 6, November 23, 2018. www.liputan6.com/news/read/3725019/ polisi-tangkap-admin-instagram-sr23-penyebar-jokowi-pki.

Quintal, Étienne. "Canada First Is Inevitable: Analyzing Youth-Oriented Far-Right Propaganda on TikTok." PhD diss., Université d'Ottawa/University of Ottawa, 2022.

Radue, Melanie. "Harmful Disinformation in Southeast Asia: "Negative Campaigning," "Information Operations" and "Racist Propaganda" – Three Forms of Manipulative Political Communication in Malaysia, Myanmar, and Thailand." *Journal of Contemporary Eastern Asia* 18, no. 2(2019). DOI: 10.17477/jcea.2019.18.2.068.

Rahayu, Lisye Sri. "Ma'ruf Amin jelaskan video viral 'Ahok sumber konflik, harus dihabisi'." *Detik*. April 4, 2019. news.detik.com/berita/d-4496391/maruf-amin-je laskan-video-viral-ahok-sumber-konflik-harus-dihabisi.

Rahim, Samsudin A. "What can we learn about social media influence in the Malaysian 14th General Election?" *Journal of Asian Pacific Communication* 29, no. 2 (2019): 264–80.

Rahman, Serina. "Was it a Malay Tsunami? Deconstructing the Malay vote in Malaysia's 2018 Election." *The Round Table* 107, no. 6 (2018): 669–82.

Rahman, Serina. "Communication Covid-19 effectively in Malaysia: Challenges and Recommendations." *Trends in Southeast Asia* 3 (2022). www.iseas.edu.sg/wp -content/uploads/2021/12/TRS3_22.pdf.

Rainsford, Keith Carr. Kuching, Sarawak, Borneo. 1945–09–14. Kuching Force. Japanese Propaganda. A Large Sign Painted on The Side of a Public Building in Kuching. September 14, 1943. www.awm.gov.au/collection/C202578.

Rakhmani, Inaya, and Sri Saraswati Muninggar. "Authoritarian Populism in Indonesia: The Role of the Political Campaign Industry in Engineering Consent and Coercion." *Journal of Current Southeast Asian Affairs* 40, no. 3 (2021): 436–60. DOI: 10.1177/18681034211027885.

Rakhmat, Muhamad Zulfikar, and Winanda Aryansyah. "Rising Anti-Chinese Sentiment in Indonesia." *The Asean Post*, July 4, 2020. theaseanpost.com/article/ rising-anti-chinese-sentiment-indonesia.

Ramadhan, Dony Indra. "Buni Yani disebut sengaja hilangkan kata 'pakai' di video Ahok." *Detiknews*, June 13, 2017. news.detik.com/berita/d-3528813/buni-yani-dis ebut-sengaja-hilangkan-kata-pakai-di-video-ahok.

Rasidi, Pradipa P., and Khoirun Nisa Sukmani. "Languages of Propaganda." *Inside Indonesia*, October 13, 2021. www.insideindonesia.org/languages-of-propaganda.

Ratkiewicz, Jacob, Michael Conover, Mark Meiss, Bruno Goncalves, Snehal Patil, Alessandro Flammini, and Filippo Menczer. "Detecting and Tracking the Spread of Astroturf Memes in Microblog Streams." arXiv, 2011. 1011.3768.

"Redam dampak virus corona, Jokowi beri influencer Rp72M." *CNN Indonesia*. February 25, 2020. www.cnnindonesia.com/ekonomi/20200225172035–532–478022/ redam-dampak-virus-corona-jokowi-beri-influencer-rp72-.

Reid, Anthony. "Jewish-Conspiracy Theories in Southeast Asia: Are Chinese the Target?" *Indonesia and the Malay World* 38, no. 112 (2010): 373–85.

Reisch, Zachary. "The Institute for Propaganda Analysis: Protecting Democracy in Pre-World War II America." PhD dissertation, 2014.

Ressa, Maria. "Propaganda War: Weaponizing the Internet." *Rappler*, October 3, 2016. www.rappler.com/nation/propaganda-war-weaponizing-internet.

Rex, Tan. "GE15 Monitor Singles Out Siti Zailah, Ganabatirau Among Candidates Resorting to Ethnoreligious Rhetoric in Campaigns." *Yahoo News*, November 8, 2022. bit.ly/3kAjCO3.

Rich, Matoko. "As Coronavirus Spreads, So Does Anti-China Sentiment." *The New York Times,* January 30, 2020. www.nytimes.com/2020/01/30/world/asia/ coronavirus-chinese-racism.html.

Rizkinaswara, Leski. "Presiden Jokowi: Literasi Digital akan Tingkatkan Kecakapan Digital Masyarakat." *Aptika Kominfo*, May 20, 2021. aptika.kominfo.go.id/2021/05 /presiden-jokowi-literasi-digital-akan-tingkatkan-kecakapan-digital-masyarakat/.

Rjéoutski, Vladislav, and Natalia Speranskaia. "The Francophone Press in Russia: A Cultural Bridge and an Instrument of Propaganda." *French and Russian in Imperial Russia* 1 (2015): 84–102.

Rogers, Everett Mitchell, and Lawrence Kincaid. *Communication Network: Toward A New Paradigm for Research*. New York: Free Press, 1981.

Romano, Angela. "Development Journalism: State Versus Practitioner Perspectives in Indonesia." *Media Asia* 26, no. 4 (2009): 183–91. DOI: 10.1080/01296612. 1999.11726592.

Ross, Sheryl Tuttle. "Understanding Propaganda: The Epistemic Merit Model and Its Application to Art." *Journal of Aesthetic Education* 36, no. 1 (2002): 16–30.

"RUU cipta kerja ancam hak asasi manusia." *Amnesty*, August 19, 2020. www .amnesty.id/ruu-cipta-kerja-ancam-hak-asasi-manusia/#:%7E:text=Amnesty %20berpendapat%2C%20secara%20substansi%2C%20RUU,Sosial%20dan %20Budaya%20(ICESCR).

Saat, Norshahril, and Afra Alatas. "Islamisation in Malaysia Beyond UMNO and PAS." *Fulcrum*. October 11, 2022. fulcrum.sg/islamisation-in-malaysia-beyond -umno-and-pas/.

Safitri, Priska Nur, Santi Indra Astuti, Nuril Hidayah, Cahya Suryani, Mizati Dewi Wasdiana, and Anita Wahid. "When Politics and Religion Become Disaster: An Annual Mapping of Hoax in Indonesia." *Ultimacomm: Jurnal Ilmu Komunikasi* 13, no. 2 (2021): 343–57.

Saleh, Salinatin Mohamad, Azahari, Mustaffa Halabi, and Ismail, Adzrool Idzwan. "Diabetic Healthcare Awareness in Malaysia: The Role of Poster as a Communication Medium." Procedia-Social and Behavioral Sciences 91 (2013): 539–44.

Samuel, Thomas Koruth. *Radicalisation in Southeast Asia: A selected case study of Daesh in Indonesia, Malaysia and the Philippines*. Southeast Asia Regional Centre for Counter-Terrorism (SEARCCT), Ministry of Foreign Affairs, 2016.

Sancaya, Rengga. "Jokowi bertemu relawan Jasmev." Detik. August 25, 2012. news. detik.com/foto-news/d-1998944/jokowi-bertemu-relawan-jasmev.

Sanders, Michael L., and Philip M. Taylor. *British Propaganda During the First World War, 1914–18*. Macmillan International Higher Education, 1982.

Sandle, Paul. "London Police and Facebook Move to Stop Live Streaming of Terror Attacks." *Reuters*. September 18, 2019. www.reuters.com/article/britain-security -facebook-idINKBN1W221Z.

Santoso, Audrey "Posting Hoax Jokowi PKI, Admin IG sr23_official Ditangkap." *Detik News*, November 23, 2018. news.detik.com/berita/d-4314237/posting-hoax-jokowi-pki-admin-ig-sr23official-ditangkap.

Sapiie, Marguerita Afra, and Agnes Anya. "Jokowi Accuses Prabowo Camp of Enlisting Foreign Propaganda Help." *The Jakarta Post*, February 4, 2019. www .thejakartapost.com/news/2019/02/04/jokowi-accuses-prabowo-camp-of-enlisting -foreign-propaganda-help.html.

Sapiie, Marguerite Afra. "Supreme Court Called on to Resolve Ex-Graft Convict Election Candidate Controversy." *The Jakarta Post*, September 6, 2018. www .thejakartapost.com/news/2018/09/05/supreme-court-called-on-to-resolve-ex-graft -convict-election-candidate-controversy.html.

Sasongko, Agung. "Video Ahok: Anda dibohongi Alquran Surat Al-Maidah 51 viral di medsos." *Republika*, October 6, 2016. www.republika.co.id/berita/oem6xe313/ video-ahok-anda-dibohongi-alquran-surat-almaidah-51-viral-di-medsos.

Scheufele, Dietram A. "Agenda-Setting, Priming, and Framing Revisited: Another Look at Cognitive Effects of Political Communication." *Mass Communication & Society* 3, no. 2–3 (2000): 297–316.

Schuldt, Lasse. "Official Truths in a War on Fake News: Governmental Fact-Checking in Malaysia, Singapore, and Thailand." *Journal of Current Southeast Asian Affairs* 40, no. 2 (2021): 340–71.

Seiff, Abby. "This Country's Election Shows the Complicated Role Twitter Plays in Democracy." *Huffpost*, May 5, 2018. www.huffpost.com/entry/twitter-malaysia -elections_n_5aeafdd5e4b00f70f0efe0bf.

"Selama 2018, Siber Kreasi Telah Menjangkau 350 Lokasi." *Kominfo*, January 18, 2019. www.kominfo.go.id/content/detail/15955/selama-2018-siber-kreasi-telah -menjangkau-350-lokasi/0/berita_satker.

Septianto, Bayu. "Polisi bubarkan demo pendukung Jerinx di depan kejari Denpasar." *Tirto*, September 29, 2020. tirto.id/polisi-bubarkan-demo-pendukung-jerinx-di-depan-kejari-denpasar-f5kf.

Shane, Scott. "The Fake Americans Russia Created to Influence the Election." *The New York Times*, September, 7, 2017. cs.brown.edu/people/jsavage/VotingProject /2017_09_07_NYT_TheFakeAmericansRussiaCreatedToInfluenceTheElection.pdf.

Shehada, Muhammad. "Recycling Israeli Propaganda Tactics to Defend Saudi Arabia." *The New Arab*, November 12, 2018. english.alaraby.co.uk/opinion/recyc ling-israeli-propaganda-tactics-defend-saudi-arabia.

Shelton, Tracy, and Iffah Nur Arifah. "Indonesian Actress and Activist Ratna Sarumpaet Lies About Political Assault to Hide Cosmetic Surgery." October 4, 2018. www.abc.net.au/news/2018–10–04/indonesian-actress-lies-about-assault-after-cosmetic-surgery/10337412.

Shepherd, Jack. "Marvel Artist Who Inserted Anti-Semitic and Anti-Christian Messages into X-Men Comic Apologises: 'My Career Is Over'." *Independent*. April 11, 2017. www.independent.co.uk/arts-entertainment/books/news/marvel-xmen-gold -1-muslim-antisemitic-antichristian-ardian-syaf-apology-a7677726.html.

Shepperd, James, Wendi Malone, and Kate Sweeny. "Exploring Causes of the Self-Serving Bias." *Social and Personality Psychology Compass* 2, no. 2 (2008): 895–908.

Sherman, Justin. "Vietnam's Internet Control: Following in China's Footsteps?" *The Diplomat*, December 11, 2019. thediplomat.com/2019/12/vietnams-internet-con trol-following-in-chinas-footsteps/.

Shifman, Limor. *Memes in Digital Culture*. The MIT Press, 2014.

Siahaan, Chontina, and Manotar Tampubolon. "Electoral Manipulation in Indonesia's 2019 National Election." *Journal of Positive Psychology & Wellbeing* 5, no. 4 (2021): 1943–55.

Sihaloha, Markus Junianto. "Pengamat: Jokowi, Tri, dan Wridwan Antitesis SBY." *Beritasatu*, October 31, 2013. www.beritasatu.com/nasional/147717/pengamat -jokowi-tri-dan-ridwan-antitesis-sby.

Sihombing, Rolando Fransiscus. "Anggota DPR singgung Yosi Project Pop Siberkreasi, ini jawaban Kominfo." *Detik*, September 2, 2020. news.detik.com/ berita/d-5156984/anggota-dpr-singgung-yosi-project-pop-siberkreasi-ini-jawaban -kominfo.

Silvestri, Lisa. "Mortars and Memes: Participating in Pop Culture from a War Zone." *Media, War, & Conflict* 9, no. 1 (2015): 27–42. DOI: 10.1177/1750635215611608.

"Siman, sinergi media sosial aparatur negara." *Jakut Kemenkumham*, November 5, 2019. rupbasan-jakut.kemenkumham.go.id/berita-utama/siman-sinergi-media-sosi al-aparatur-negara

Simon, Sheldon W. "President Bush Presses Antiterror Agenda in Southeast Asia." *Comparative Connections* 5, no. 4 (2004): 67–77.

Sinaga, Dames Alexander, Alin Almanar, and Novi Setuningsih. "Gov't Officially Disbands Hizbut Tahrir Indonesia." *Jakarta Globe*, July 19, 2017. jakartaglobe.id/context/govt-officially-disbands-hizbut-tahrir-indonesia.

"Sinergi media sosial aparatur sipil negara solusi pemerintah berantas hoax." *Jabar Kemkumham*, May 25, 2018. jabar.kemenkumham.go.id/berita-kanwil/berita-utama/sinergi-media-sosial-aparatur-sipil-negara-solusi-pemerintah-berantas-hoax.

Singapore Internal Security Department. Singapore Terrorism Threat Assessment Report 2021. Accessed April 1, 2022. www.mha.gov.sg/docs/default-source/default-document-library/singapore-terrorism-threat-assessment-report-2021.pdf.

Singh, Jasminder, and Muhammad Haziq Bin Jani. ""Daesh-isation" of Southeast Asia's Jihadists." *RSIS Commentaries* 80 (2016).

Sinha, G. Alex. "Lies, Gaslighting and Propaganda." *Buffalo Law Review* 68, no. 1037 (2020). digitalcommons.law.buffalo.edu/buffalolawreview/vol68/iss4/3.

Skidmore, Max J. "Populism and Its Perils: Language and Politics." *Annales Universitatis Mariae Curie-Skłodowska, sectio K-Politologia* 22, no. 1 (2016): 7.

Smith, Blake. "Indonesians Hate the Chinese, Because They Are Jewish." *TableMag*, April 16, 2018. www.tabletmag.com/sections/arts-letters/articles/indonesians-hate-the-chinese-because-they-are-jewish.

Soeriaatmadja, Wahyudi, and Francis Chan. "6 Killed, 200 Injured in Jakarta Election Protests That Police Say Are 'by Design'." *The Straits Times*, May 23, 2019. www.straitstimes.com/asia/se-asia/security-forces-use-tear-gas-to-disperse-small-groups-of-rioters-in-jakarta.

Soong, Kua Kia. "Racial Conflict in Malaysia: Against the Official History." *Race & Class* 49, no. 3 (2008): 33–53.

Souisa, Hellena. "Misinformation, Ratna the Hoaxer, and 1965." *Indonesia at Melbourne*, October 8, 2018. indonesiaatmelbourne.unimelb.edu.au/fake-news-ratna-the-hoaxer-and-1965/.

Sparkes-Vian, Cassian. "Digital Propaganda: The Tyranny of Ignorance." *Critical Sociology* 45, no. 3 (2018): 1–17. DOI: 10.177/0896920517754241.

Sriramesh, Krihsnamurty. "Public Relations Practice and Research in Asia: A Conceptual Framework." In *Public Relations in Asia: An Anthology*, edited by Krishnamurty Sriramesh. Singapore: Thomson Learning, 2004.

Stephan, Walter G., David Rosenfield, and Cookie Stephan. "Egotism in Males and Females." *Journal of Personality and Social Psychology* 34, no. 6 (1976): 1161.

Strangio, Sebastian. "Indonesia's Parliament Passes Repressive New Penal Code." *The Diplomat*, December 6, 2022. thediplomat.com/2022/12/indonesias-parliament-passes-repressive-new-penal-code/.

Strick, Benjamin, and Famega Syavira. "Papua Unrest: Social Media Bots Skewing the Narrative." *BBC*, October 11, 2019. www.bbc.com/news/world-asia-49983667.

"Struktur organisasi." Perhumas. Accessed July 9, 2022. www.perhumas.or.id/struktur-organisasi/.

Suaedy, Ahmad. "The Role of Volunteers and Political Participation in the 2012 Jakarta Gubernatorial Election." *Journal of Current Southeast Asian Affairs* 33, no. 1 (2014): 111–38. DOI: 10.1177/186810341403300106.

Sualman, Ismail, Nuurrianti Jalli, Razween Rashidi, and Yuliandre Darwis. "An Analysis of Cultural Elements in Selected Festive Advertisements." *Malaysian Journal of Communication*, no. 37 (2021): 334–47.

Sulaiman, Noor Atiqah. "Umno the Real Extremist, Not PN, Says Lau." *New Straits Times*, 24 December 2022. www.nst.com.my/news/politics/2022/12/864261/umno -real-extremist-not-pn-says-lau

Sumari, Arwin Datumaya Wahyudi. "Urgensi sinergi media sosial aparatur negara." *Researchgate*. Accessed July 9, 2021, www.researchgate.net/publication /330839646_Urgensi_Sinergi_Media_Sosial_Aparatur_Negara.

Sunaryo, Arie. "Jokowi soal usul percepatan pelantikan: Yang punya kerja itu MPR, jangan tanya saya." *Merdeka*, October 2, 2019. www.merdeka.com/politik /jokowi-soal-usul-percepatan-pelantikan-yang-punya-kerja-itu-mpr-jangan-tanya -saya.html.

Suryadinata, Leo. "New Chinese Migrants in Indonesia: An Emerging Community That Faces New Challenges." *Perspective*, June 11, 2020. www.iseas.edu.sg/wp -content/uploads/2020/04/ISEAS_Perspective_2020_61.pdf.

Susanto, Billy Shaw. "The Evolution of Communication and Why Stickers Matter." *Forbes*, July 31, 2018. www.forbes.com/sites/forbestechcouncil/2018/07/31/the -evolution-of-communication-and-why-stickers-matter/?sh=568945062b2f.

Sutan, Arissy Jorgi, Achmad Nurmandi, Dyah Mutiarin, and Salahudin Salahudin. "Using Social Media as Tools of Social Movement and Social Protest in Omnibus Law of Job Creation Bill Policy-Making Process in Indonesia." In *International Conference on Advances in Digital Science*, 261–74. Cham: Springer, 2021.

Symons-Brown, Bonny, and Matt Henry. 2022. "The Marcos Makeover: How History was Rewritten to Place a Dictator's Son on the Cusp of Power." *ABC News*, May 5, 2022. www.abc.net.au/news/2022–05–05/bongbong-marcos-philippines-election-social-media/101035620.

Tambun, Lenny Tristia. "Undang influencer, istana sebut Jokowi ingin kenal dekat dengan semua stakeholder." *Berita Satu*, August 21, 2020. www.beritasatu.com /politik/667941/undang-influencer-istana-sebut-jokowi-ingin-kenal-dekat-dengan -semua-stakeholder.

Tan, Netina. "Electoral Management of Digital Campaigns and Disinformation in East and Southeast Asia." *Election Law Journal: Rules, Politics, and Policy* 19, no. 2 (2020): 214–39.

Tapsell, Ross. "The Polarisation Paradox in Indonesia's 2019 Elections." *New Mandala*, March 22, 2019. www.newmandala.org/the-polarisation-paradox-in -indonesias-2019-elections/.

Tapsell, Ross. "The Smartphone as the 'Weapon of the Weak': Assessing the Role of Communication Technologies in Malaysia's Regime Change." *Journal of Current Southeast Asian Affairs* 7, no. 3 (2019): 9–29.

Tee, Kenneth. "Law Minister Confirms Emergency Ended in Aug, But Says Ordinances Still Apply Until Feb 2022." *Malay Mail*, October 21, 2021. www .malaymail.com/news/malaysia/2021/10/01/law-minister-confirms-emergency -ended-in-aug-but-says-ordinances-still-appl/2009806.

"Terawan sebut ekstrak temu lawak dan ikan gabus suplemen covid." *CNN Indonesia*, July 14, 2020. www.cnnindonesia.com/nasional/20200714223737–20–524738/terawan-sebut-ekstrak-temulawak-dan-ikan-gabus-suplemen-covid.

"The World in 2050." PWC. www.pwc.com/gx/en/issues/economy/the-world-in-2050.html.

Thien, Vee Vian. "The Struggle for Digital Freedom of Speech." *Access Contested Security, Identity, Resistance in Asian Cyberspace* (2011): 43–46.

TikTok. "TikTok community guidelines." Accessed April 18, 2022, www.tiktok.com/community-guidelines?lang=en#37.

Tim Merdeka. "Motif tukang batagir bikin hoaks serbuan TKA China di Morowali terungkap." *Merdeka*, January 30, 2019. www.merdeka.com/peristiwa/motif-tukang-batagor-bikin-hoaks-serbuan-tka-china-di-morowali-terungkap.html.

Tiung, Lee Kuok, Rizal Zamani Idris, and Rafiq Idris. "Propaganda dan disinformasi: politik persepsi dalam pilihan raya umum ke-14 (pru-14) Malaysia: Propaganda and Disinformation: Politics of Perception in Malaysian's 14th General Election (GE-14)." *Jurnal Kinabalu* (2018): 171–71.

Tsalikis, Catherine. "Maria Ressa: 'Facebook Broke Democracy in Many Countries Around the World, Including in Mine'." *Center for International Governance Innovation* (2019).

U.S. Department of State. "2021 Report in International Religious Freedom: Malaysia." June 6, 2022. www.state.gov/reports/2021-report-on-international-religious-freedom/malaysia/.

Vallier, Ivan. "The Roman Catholic Church: A Transnational Actor." *International Organization* 25, no. 3 (1971): 479–502. www.jstor.org/stable/2706052.

Varkkey, Helena. "Emergent Geographies of Chronic Air Pollution Governance in Southeast Asia: Transboundary Publics in Singapore." *Environmental Policy and Governance* (2022).

Vaswani, Karishma. "Joko Jokowi Wins Indonesia Presidential Election." *BBC*, July 22, 2014. www.bbc.com/news/world-asia-28415536.

Wahyuni, Nungki, and Dinh Mai Nguyet. "Hoax and Provocative Contents by Muslim Cyber Army (MCA) and Its Enforcement in Indonesia." *Indonesian Journal of Counter Terrorism and National Security* 1, no. 1 (2022): 67–90.

Walzer, Arthur. "Faking the News: What Rhetoric Can Teach Us About Donald J. Trump." In *Rhetoric Society Quarterly*, edited by Ryan Skinnell, 49, no. 2 (2018): 209–12. DOI: 10.1080/02773945.2018.1540208.

Wanawir, Wanawir, Lisdwiana Kurniati, Umi Kholidah, and Ainur Rosidah. "Critical Discourse Analysis Online News 'Omnibus Law' Job Creation Case (Teun A. Van Dijk Model)." - (2020): 1–13.

Wanless, Alicia, and Michael Berk. "Participatory Propaganda: The Engagement of Audiences in the Spread of Persuasion Communication." *Proceedings of the Social Media and Social Order, Culture Conflict 2.0 Conference* 2017. www.researchgate.net/profile/Alicia-Wanless/publication/.

Warburton, Eve. "Deepening Polarization and Democratic Decline in Indonesia." In *Political Polarization in South and Southeast Asia: Old Divisions, New Dangers,*

edited by Thomas Carothers, and Andrew O'Donohue. August 18, 2020. carne
gieendowment.org/2020/08/18/deepening-polarization-and-democratic-decline-in-
indonesia-pub-82435.

Warburton, Eve. "Polarisation in Indonesia: What if Perception Is Reality?" *New
Mandala*, April 16, 2019. www.newmandala.org/how-polarised-is-indonesia/.

Wardle, Claire, and Hossein Derakshan. "Thinking About 'Information Disorder': For-
mats of Misinformation, Disinformation, and Mal-Information." *Journalism, Fake
News, and Disinformation*. 2018. unesdoc.unesco.org/ark:/48223/pf0000265552.

Wardle, Claire, and Hossein Derakhshan. *Information Disorder: Toward an Interdis-
ciplinary Frame for Research and Policy Making*. Council of Europe, 2017.

"Warganet diajak melawan kampanye negatif asing soal sawit." *rctiplus*. September
17, 2019. www.rctiplus.com/news/detail/73010/warganet-diajak-melawan
-kampanye-negatif-asing-soal-sawit.

Weaver, David, Maxwell McCombs, and Donald L. Shaw. "Agenda-Setting Research:
Issues, Attributes, and Influences." *Handbook of Political Communication Research*
(2004): 275–300.

Webster, James. *The Martketplace od Attention: How Audiences Take Shape in a
Digital Age*. MIT Press, 2014.

Wieringa, Saskia E., and Nursyahbani Katjasungkana. *Propaganda and the Genocide
in Indonesia: Imagined Evil*. Routledge, 2018.

Wijaya, Callistasia Anggun. "Ahok Speech Uploader Questioned Over Defamation
Claims." *The Jakarta Post*, November 18, 2016. www.thejakartapost.com/news
/2016/11/18/ahok-speech-uploader-questioned-over-defamation-claims.html.

Wijayanto and Maizar Albanik. "Cyber mercenaries vs the KPK." *Inside Indonesia*,
October 13, 2021. www.insideindonesia.org/cyber-mercenaries-vs-the-kpk.

Wijayanto and Ward Berenschot. "Organisation and Funding of Social Media
Propaganda." *Inside Indonesia*, October 31, 2021. www.insideindonesia.org/
organisation-and-funding-of-social-media-propaganda.

Wilson, Steven Lloyd, and Charles Wiysonge. "Social Media and Vaccine Hesitancy."
BMJ Global Health 5, no. 10 (2020): e004206.

Winters, Jefferey. A. "Oligarchy and Democracy in Indonesia." *Indonesia* 96 (2013):
11–33. DOI: 10.5728/indonesia.96.0099.

Wise, Jamie. "Cambodia 'Fake News' Laws Tightened Noose on Press Freedom."
International Press Institute, October 1, 2019. ipi.media/cambodia-fake-news-laws
-tighten-noose-on-press-freedom/.

"Wishnutama rinci dana Rp72 M buat wisata, termasuk Influencer." *CNN Indonesia*, February 26, 2020. www.cnnindonesia.com/ekonomi/20200226174101–532–478425/
wishnutama-rinci-dana-rp72-m-buat-wisata-termasuk-influencer.

Wolfowitz, Paul. "Indonesia Is a Model Muslim Democracy." American Enterprise
Institute, July 17, 2009. www.aei.org/articles/indonesia-is-a-model-muslim
-democracy/.

Wong, Vicky. "In Pictures: Hong Kong's Political Messaging App Stickers
Explained." *Hong Kong Free Press*, August 7, 2015. hongkongfp.com/2015/08/07
/in-pictures-hong-kongs-political-messaging-app-stickers-explained/.

Yatid, Moonyati Mohd. "Truth Tampering Through Social Media Malaysia's Approach in Fighting Disinformation and Misinformation." 2019. pssat.ugm.ac.id /wp-content/uploads/sites/513/2019/03/Paper-4.pdf.

Yuwita, Nurma. "Representasi Nasionalisme Dalam Film Rudy Habibie (Studi Analisis Semiotika Charles Sanders Pierce)." *Jurnal Heritage* 6, no. 1 (2018): 40–48.

Zahid, Syed Jaymal. "In Yet Another Rant Against DAP, Hadi Accuses Party of Spreading Islamophobia." The Malay Mail, November 28, 2022. www.malaymail.com/news/malaysia/2022/11/28/in-yet-another-rant-against-dap-hadi-accuses -party-of-spreading-islamophobia/42305.

Zainal Anuar, Mohamad Zamri, and Nuurianti Jalli. "'Malu Apa Bossku?' Najib Razak's Political Rhetoric on Facebook Post 2018 General Election." *Forum Komunikasi (FK)* 15, no 1 (2020): 1–29. ISSN 0128–2379 forumkomunikasi.uitm.edu.my.

Zhang, Xin, Xiaoyan Ding, and Liang Ma. "The Influences of Information Overload and Social Overload on Intention to Switch in Social Media." *Behaviour & Information Technology* 41, no. 2 (2022): 228–41.

Index

Note: Page numbers in italics refer to figures and tables.

About the Authors

Nuurrianti Jalli serves as an assistant professor of Professional Practice at Oklahoma State University. Hailing from Malaysia, she pursued her doctoral degree in Mass Communication at Ohio University, honing her expertise in the field.

Nuurrianti's research ambitiously addresses complex themes such as information disorders, media literacy, open-source intelligence, and the interplay between media and democracy in Southeast Asia. Her impactful collaborations with global institutions, including the United Nations, UNESCO, Brookings Institution, Konrad Adenauer Stiftung, DoubleThink Lab, and ByteDance (TikTok), illustrate the wide recognition of her work.

Not limited to academia, Nuurrianti's influence extends to the public sector, where she leverages her expertise as a communication and media consultant. In this capacity, she has provided critical advice to several Malaysian government agencies, such as the Ministry of Tourism, Arts, and Culture (MOTAC), the Community Communication Department, the Prime Minister's Office, and the Sarawak State Government.

Throughout her career, Nuurrianti has consistently shown a commitment to the application of rigorous research to practical policy issues, embodying the bridge between academic knowledge and real-world solutions.

Ika Idris, an associate professor at the Public Policy and Management program at Monash University, Indonesia, also chairs the Monash Climate Change Communication Research Hub-Indonesia Node. Specializing in social media analytics, she was a researcher at Ohio University's SMARTLab and the first non-US fellow to train at Texas State University's PhD Digital Bootcamp. In 2023, she joined the Resilience Network to combat disinformation in Indonesia.

Previously, Ika served as Director of Research at Universitas Paramadina's Public Policy Institute and an assistant professor at its Graduate School of Communication. Her interests span social media analytics, government communication, digital platforms' policies, and digital literacy.

A proponent of strategic communication for public policy and service delivery, Ika has consulted various government agencies on policy implementation and evaluation. Her notable projects include stakeholder analysis for the Indonesian Corruption Eradication Commission, service evaluations for Jakarta's Provincial Government, and curriculum development for government public relations training.

Since 2019, she has provided training on strategic public communication and social media analysis to diverse governmental bodies, aiding in the development of the nation's digital literacy and strategic communication capabilities.

www.ingramcontent.com/pod-product-compliance
Lightning Source LLC
Chambersburg PA
CBHW062033270326
41929CB00014B/2415